The Sociologically Examined Life

PIECES OF THE CONVERSATION

Michael Schwalbe

North Carolina State University

Mayfield Publishing Company

Mountain View, California
London ▪ Toronto

Library of Congress Cataloging-in-Publication Data
Schwalbe, Michael.
    The sociologically examined life : pieces of the
conversation / Michael Schwalbe.
        p.   cm.
    ISBN 1-55934-931-X
    1. Sociology—Methodology. 2. Sociology—
Philosophy. I. Title.
HM24.S3757 1997
301'.01—dc21   97-27097
                                     CIP

Manufactured in the United States of America
10   9   8   7   6   5   4   3

Mayfield Publishing Company
1280 Villa Street
Mountain View, CA 94041

Sponsoring editor, Serina Beauparlant; *production editor,*
Julianna Scott Fein; *design manager,* Jean Mailander; *text
designer,* Lisa Mirski Devenish; *cover designer,* Laurie
Anderson; *manufacturing manager,* Randy Hurst. The text
was set in 10/13 Tiepolo Book by ExecuStaff and printed
on 50# Butte des Morts by Banta Book Group.

■ ■ ■ ■ ■ ■ ■ ■

The usual introductory text imparts a lot of facts and ideas but doesn't do a very good job of teaching students how to think sociologically, and that, more than anything, is what I try to get my students to do. My struggle in this respect has led me to write *The Sociologically Examined Life: Pieces of the Conversation*. I've half-jokingly called it an "anti-text," meaning that I want it to be everything that those ponderous hardcover texts are not: readable, provocative, personal, and ethically challenging. Through this book I'm trying to gently yet firmly teach readers how to think sociologically. In the tradition of Peter Berger (*Invitation to Sociology*) and C. Wright Mills (*The Sociological Imagination*), I believe that this requires not only a change in consciousness, but also a change in how we live.

When standard introductory texts include a chapter on "the sociological perspective," the chapter usually boils down to either a list of concepts or a tip-of-the-iceberg account of sociology's conventional trinity: functionalism, conflict theory, and symbolic interactionism. I suspect that this standard fare leaves many students wondering how, if at all, everyday life looks different if you come at it sociologically. Here I try to get this across by deemphasizing the institutional discipline of sociology. Instead of saying, "Sociologists think such and such about so and so," as if students should care about what sociologists think, I simply jump into the work of taking the social world apart sociologically. Rather than display the contents of our shiny intellectual toolbox, I try to put the tools to use.

The risk in this approach is that some teachers of sociology won't like how I've chosen to take things apart. Courting that risk—and I don't see how I could avoid it and still write an honest book—is another reason I've thought of *The Sociologically Examined Life* as an anti-text. Most texts play it pretty safe, not pushing the implications of sociological thinking to the point of arousing much discomfort. My goal is certainly not to provoke for the sake of provoking, but nor have I tried to play it safe to make the book palatable to all political tastes. Many of the analyses here treat American society quite critically, and I'm sure this is going to bother some folks.

My hope is that the bother will be productive. I'd like this book to spark conversations between teachers and students and among students themselves. My examples and analyses are intended to stir thoughts and feelings that will impel discussion. In this sense, I think that *The Sociologically Examined Life* will appeal to teachers who want serious interaction with students, even if this means working through some disagreements. It seems to me that that's what intellectual conversation is about, and that whatever gets us into such conversations offers us a chance to move toward better understanding, and ultimately changing, the world we live in.

Much of the help I had in writing this book came before I sat down to do it. I could make a long list of the people who taught me—in the classroom, in print, and in conversation—and the list would be hopelessly incomplete (see chapter 4 on the social nature of individual lives). Perhaps all I can do is to offer a wide, beaming gratitude to all the minds—within and beyond the sociological universe—whose thoughts have informed my own.

I can, however, be more specific about the people who helped during the process of writing. My editor at Mayfield, Serina Beauparlant, was an unflagging supporter, even when I was being a difficult author. I am also indebted to Serina for her willingness to take risks with this project and hope that the debt ends up being repaid many times over. I owe thanks to a slew of reviewers whose comments helped me to nip and tuck the manuscript into better shape. The reviewers included Peter Adler, University of Denver; Chet Ballard, Valdosta State University; Conrad L. Kanagy, Elizabethtown College; Donileen Loseke, University of South Florida; Claus Mueller, City University of New York–Hunter College; Laura E. Nathan, Mills College; Samuel M. Richards, Penn State University; Rik Scarce, Montana State University; Rhonda Singer, Smith College; Clifford L. Staples, University of North Dakota; Vegavahini Subramaniam, Western Washington University; and Becky Thompson, Simmons College. Other colleagues who gave helpful feedback on chapters include Daphne Holden, Sandra Godwin, Doug Mason-Schrock, and Paula England. Thanks to you all.

My deepest thanks go to my partner, Sherryl Kleinman, who helped me to maintain a consistent voice throughout the text and a clear sense of purpose while I was writing. I am grateful, too, for her help in becoming more mindful of the patterns and connections that constitute our lives as social beings and, especially, our life together.

CONTENTS
■■■■■■■■■■

Preface   v

CHAPTER 1
Making Sense of the World Differently   1

CHAPTER 2
The Social World As a Human Invention   11

CHAPTER 3
Seeing Connections   27

CHAPTER 4
The Social Nature of Individual Lives   43

CHAPTER 5
Becoming Human   63

CHAPTER 6
Behavior As a Product of Circumstance   81

CHAPTER 7
Seeing Patterns   101

CHAPTER 8
Contingency and Cause　115

CHAPTER 9
Images, Representations, and Accounts　137

CHAPTER 10
Understanding Power in Social Life　153

CHAPTER 11
How to Tell Differences from Inequalities　173

CHAPTER 12
Finding Out How the Social World Works　193

CHAPTER ONE

Making Sense of the World Differently

Not much was happening in the shoe department. Elsewhere in the store people fussed over backpacks, tents, plastic kayaks, and other outdoor gear. But the two young men who sold hiking boots were enjoying a break. I was a few feet away, looking at hats, and could hear their conversation. One of them, leaning back against the counter, arms folded across his chest, was telling his coworker about college.

"It was a lot of fun," he said, "but I didn't learn anything I didn't already know."

"Yeah?" said his partner, a bit of wonderment in his voice.

"Yeah, my business communication class was good. We learned how to write memos. But most of the rest of it, pretty much all my classes—it was all just common sense. If it wasn't for getting the degree, it would have been a waste of time."

Hearing this took my mind off the hats. I imagined asking the young man how he had gotten so smart at 18 that he could listen to professors and read books for four years and not learn anything new. I wanted to puncture his arrogance and scold him for wasting the time of those who had tried to teach him. Other college professors might have felt the same way.

My anger faded as I realized that the boaster could not have meant what he said. Surely he had learned *something* in college. So what was he saying? Perhaps he belittled his education because he was angry that it hadn't gotten him a better job. Or perhaps he was trying to say to his buddy, "I'm no better than you for having gone to college. Common sense is what matters." If this is what he meant, it was not such a bad message.

Still, I was sad that he spoke of his education as a waste. Even if he had learned more than he realized, he had also missed a lot. He had not learned how to look back on himself, how to see who he was, what he was becoming, and how he was connected to others. If he had, perhaps he could have explained, without making his buddy feel bad, how his education had benefited him.

I do not suppose that courses in memo writing or other technical subjects are likely to foster much self-awareness. That is not their purpose. But other kinds of courses, and whole fields of study, claim this purpose as their reason for being. My own field of study, sociology, is often justified on the grounds that it helps people gain insight into themselves and into society, so they can live more satisfying, self-determined, and responsible lives. If sociology, or any discipline, can do this for people, then I think it has good reasons for being.

Yet sociology courses sometimes foster less self-awareness and insight into society than sociology promises to deliver. This failure is most likely to occur, it seems to me, when courses aim primarily to teach about sociology as a discipline: "See how scientific we are? See all these theories and concepts and findings? You had better be impressed by all this!" No teacher says these things in quite this way, of course, but sometimes this is the message that comes through. Perhaps you have heard it yourself.

When sociology is taught as a body of work created by strangers, it can seem like an exotic and fanciful thing—something that one can take or leave, depending on how interesting it is to listen in on the sayings of sociologists. If this is how sociology comes across, most people will tune it out before long. After all, what sociologists say among themselves is less interesting than social life itself. Most people, sensibly enough, would rather pay attention to social life than to the academic study of social life.

And so it often happens that an encounter with sociology leaves only a faint impression. A few scattered facts and concepts are re-membered, but there are no changed habits of mind, no well-learned ways of making a different kind of sense of the social world. It is as if, after so much telling about the pictures that others have made, we have forgotten that the point is to teach people how to make pictures for themselves.

If you would like a written portrait of the discipline of sociology, you can find one in many places—but not here. This book is not about the concepts, theories, and findings of sociology, although it makes implicit use of these. It is about how to think sociologically and about why this is worth doing. It tells and shows how to pay attention to and make sense of the social world in a sociological way. I call this the practice of being sociologically mindful. Once you master this practice, you can make the pictures for yourself.

Sociological Mindfulness

Do you recognize the typefaces used in this book? In what style is it bound? On what kind of paper is it printed? If such questions seem strange, it is because you have not learned to practice a certain kind of mindfulness with regard to books. It is the same with many things around us, familiar things that affect us deeply. We fail to see what they are because we lack the necessary kind of mindfulness. Fortunately, we can learn.

Mindfulness is more than paying attention. To be mindful of a thing is to see and appreciate its unique qualities. For example, to be mindful of a person is not just to be aware of and pay attention to that person. To be mindful of a person, as a human being, means trying to see and appreciate his or her uniqueness as a thinking and feeling being. When we are mindful of a person in this way, we see past stereotypes and prejudices.

Children often see things with amazing clarity because their minds are fresh and the world is new and wondrous to them. A child's mindfulness, however, is indiscriminate, as if one kind of grasp can get ahold of everything. As adults we learn to be mindful in ways that suit the things we encounter. We learn that people, for example, must be understood in terms of what makes them people: ideas, feelings, desires, bodies, and habits. Likewise, books must be appreciated for what makes them books: words, paper, design, binding, and so on. For each kind of thing we learn a different way of grasping it.

Sociological mindfulness is the practice of tuning-in to how the social world works. We are all tuned-in to some extent, of course, just by being members of society. But to be truly mindful of the social world we must learn to see it for what it is. We must learn, in other words, the ideas necessary to see what makes the social world a unique phenomenon. These are ideas about *how to pay attention* to the social world. Sociological mindfulness is the practice of paying attention in these ways.

What do we see if we practice sociological mindfulness? We see, for example, how the social world is created by people; how infants become functional human beings; how we are interdependent with others; how people's behavior is a response to the conditions under which they live; how social life consists of patterns within patterns; how contingencies shape our fates; how appearances are strategically crafted; how power is exercised; how inequalities are created and maintained; and how we can create valid and reliable knowledge about the social world.

A Justification for Sociological Mindfulness

Why bother to be sociologically mindful? What is the point of all this analytic thinking about social life? My answers to these questions are based on three beliefs.

The first is that a good life—one that is stimulating, intense, joyful, purposeful, caring, and dignified—can be had only in a society that is peaceful, cooperative, egalitarian, and minimally regimented. My second belief is that everyone has an equal right to a good life, and so no one should enjoy power and privilege at the expense of others. My third belief is that because human lives are intertwined, we are all obliged to consider how our actions affect others, especially their chances of living a good life.

I hope you find these beliefs reasonable as starting points. If you want to mull them over, here is an angle from which to do so. Think of the people you love and the kind of life you wish for them to have. Is it a life of violence, deprivation, and suffering, or is it something more like my vision of a good life? If it is the latter, then I hope you will consider the possibility that mindfulness may be useful as a way to create better lives for more people.

Mindfulness is useful because it helps us see *how* our lives are intertwined and how our words and deeds help or harm others in non-obvious ways. Being sociologically mindful is especially important for helping us see that the consequences of our words and deeds often escape our intentions.

For example, a person who tells a racist joke may intend only to be funny. Yet what this person does is to reinforce beliefs that some kinds of people are stupid, vain, immoral, or inferior. Even if no one is offended when the joke is told, in the long run people can be hurt. The sentiments expressed in the joke might decrease sensitivity to others' feelings and to their needs for help. Or it might be that the joke makes others seem unworthy of friendship, thus cutting people off from each other. The harm, in other words, can be indirect, subtle, and delayed. It doesn't matter that no harm was intended. It can happen nonetheless.

Harm can arise even when our actions seem honorable. For example, working hard at one's job is usually a good thing to do. But when people work for companies that make weapons, cigarettes, or pornography, or when they work for companies that advertise, sell, or defend such products, violence, death, disease, and misery are the ultimate results. No one may intend others to be hurt, yet that is what happens, and those who make it happen are responsible. The harm could not happen if not for their hard work.

The kind of awareness that sociological mindfulness produces can be unsettling because it sometimes forces us to see things we would prefer not to. But by failing to be mindful, we can inadvertently damage or destroy what we would like to preserve. Or we might, through short-sighted action, diminish our own and others' chances of living good lives. By helping us see beyond our intentions to the consequences of our actions, sociological mindfulness can help us avoid traps like these, though it does not make them easy to escape.

Being sociologically mindful also means paying attention to the hardships and options other people face. If we understand how others' circumstances differ from ours, we are more likely to show compassion for them and to grant them the respect they deserve as human beings. We are also less likely to condemn them unfairly for doing things we dislike. By helping us appreciate the conditions under which others act, sociological mindfulness can help decrease the amount of hatred and conflict in the world.

Being caught up in our daily concerns, we often fail to see and appreciate all of our connections to others—to those who make our clothes, grow our food, clean up our messes, pay for the schools we use, use the schools we pay for, benefit or suffer from actions by politicians we elect, look to us as examples, and so on. Sociological mindfulness helps us see these threads of social life and how they sustain and obligate us. The main benefit of this awareness is that it can make us more responsible members of a human community. That seems to be as good a reason as any for learning a new intellectual practice.

The Rarity of Sociological Mindfulness

If sociological mindfulness were common, I wouldn't need to argue for it. You would simply take it for granted that we all need to be aware of and to think carefully about how the social world works. You would probably think it strange for anyone to make a big deal about doing so. But it seems that sociological mindfulness is actually quite rare in our society.

One reason might be that sociological mindfulness doesn't seem like much fun. Who wants more rules for how to think? As soon as there are rules, then we must worry about getting it right or wrong. So we might feel like saying, "Enough with fancy intellectual schemes! I'm doing just fine with common sense, thank you. Besides, I would prefer to live life rather than analyze it to death." This sentiment is not unreasonable in a society where we are constantly being offered ideas of dubious merit.

Another reason that sociological mindfulness is rare might be a belief that it won't matter. Why bother thinking analytically about social life if doing so won't make a difference? Some smart and caring people withdraw from the world because they do not believe they can do anything to change it. They feel powerless, as do many people in our society. I think this is what really impedes sociological mindfulness. We tend to be mindful of things that we feel responsible for and have some control over. But if we feel powerless to change a situation, we probably won't try to analyze it deeply. We might feel lucky just to avoid trouble.

American individualism also inhibits sociological mindfulness. As Americans we learn that it is good to be self-reliant, to achieve on our own, and to look out for ourselves. Under some conditions these are helpful ideas. But they can also blind us to our interdependence with others, and to an understanding of how our ties to others lead us to think, feel, and behave in certain ways. Ideas that lead us to think of ourselves solely as competing individuals, free to do anything we want at any time, can keep us from being mindful of the social world in which we are immersed.

It is also possible that a desire for money and status may so preoccupy us that we fail to think much about how society works or how other people experience it. Or we might fear the loss of security that can come from questioning the beliefs we grew up with. Or we might be so angry at those who abuse us that we lose all sympathy for others who are worse off. Or perhaps we prefer not to reflect on how we participate in oppressing others, because it would make us feel guilty or sad.

People resist being sociologically mindful for many reasons, but not because they are naturally selfish, competitive, or cowardly. If such feelings arise and inhibit sociological mindfulness, it is because of how people have grown up. In a less competitive society where good jobs were available for everyone, people could feel more secure and would probably be willing to spend more time reflecting on how society works. When it seems like life is a race, few people may want to stop to analyze what all the racing is about or where it is leading, lest they fall behind.

Being sociologically mindful goes against the grain in Western society. It may also go against many of the impulses that have been instilled in us as Americans. How can these resistances be overcome? With ideas, first of all, since people must think it is worthwhile to practice sociological mindfulness. I hope that the ideas I have offered so far have persuaded you, at least partly, if you needed persuading.

Here is one more idea that might nudge you toward more mindfulness: Even if you are young now, you will probably die in 40 to 60 years; if you are older, you have fewer years remaining. The time will pass quickly. How do you want to use it? You could try to acquire as much wealth and fame as possible. That seems to be the main ambition for many people in our culture; there are, however, other goals for a human life. You could try to enrich the lives of others by teaching, creating art, restoring a piece of the earth, promoting health, resisting violence, or organizing for change. The question is, What kind of mark do you want to leave on the earth for having lived? If you would like to leave the earth a better place than you found it, sociological mindfulness will help you see what needs to be done.

A Continuing Conversation

No matter how carefully we study the social world, our knowledge of it is always incomplete. Even if you could read about everything, there would still be experiences that remained foreign to you. And even if you could read and experience far more than the average person, you would still be interpreting everything from your particular point of view—a view shaped by your upbringing in a particular place, time, culture, and community. There is no way around this constraint on our knowledge.

Because people see and experience different things in life, and have different ways of interpreting what they see and experience, people are bound to disagree about how the social world works and about how it ought to work. What then? If the disagreements concern matters of taste ("You *like* opera? Yecch!") or are trivial, then perhaps we can just shrug them off. "No big deal," we might say, as we wonder how it is that other people can embrace such odd notions.

Other times there is more at stake. One person might think that democracy is ensured by elections in which the candidate who gets the most votes wins a place in government, and the loser can try again next time. Another person might think that such a system is undemocratic, because it means that 49 percent of the people can end up with no voice in government. A disagreement such as this, when it involves a large number of people who have taken up sides, can lead to violent conflict.

Being sociologically mindful can help us to avoid the destructive potential of disagreements over matters large and small. If we are mindful, we will realize that our knowledge is always limited, that others know what the world looks like from where *they* stand, and that we cannot claim to have a monopoly on the truth. So at the very least we will want to listen to others and try to understand how and why they have a different view of things. We will also want to look back at ourselves and try to figure out where our knowledge has come from.

Being sociologically mindful is thus likely to engage us in a conversation aimed at understanding several important matters: how the social world works, how and why others are different from and similar to us, and how we can get along with others despite our differences. As long as we are engaged in such a conversation—as long as we are thinking, talking, and trying to understand each other and ourselves—we will not be beating anyone over the head and insisting that they do what we say. Nor will they be doing this to us.

The kind of conversation I am referring to can involve many people and can be carried on through print and other media, as well as through talk. It can also occur over long stretches of time—days, weeks, years. In fact, if we are lucky, this conversation will go on indefinitely, because that is the only way we can avoid violence and work together to create social arrangements that will allow as many people as possible to live good lives. Practicing sociological mindfulness is a way into this conversation and a way to keep it going.

This book is part of the conversation, and no serious conversation about how the social world works, or how best to make sense of it, proceeds without disagreements. And so I am sure that you will disagree with some things I say here. When this happens, please talk back to the book and raise questions, in your own mind and with others. Disagreement can move a conversation ahead if we take it as an opportunity to look more deeply into why others see the world differently. I hope that whatever disagreements this book might provoke can be used in this way.

At the end of each chapter I list a few sources at which you might want to look. These are not sources that "prove me right." They are relevant pieces of the conversation—pieces upon which I have drawn and from which you might also benefit, if you care to consult them. If you do, you will see where some of my thinking comes from, how it is a response to what has been said before, and how my thinking goes its own way. This will give you a larger view of the conversation to which this book, and now you, belongs.

All I can do in these pages is to invite you to consider a way of thinking that I believe holds great promise for making better sense of the social world and for living in it more humanely. I hope you will agree that sociological mindfulness is useful for these purposes. If I didn't believe this myself, I would not have written this book. But whatever you think, I will be satisfied if you are willing to keep the conversation going. Sometimes that is the best we can do, and sometimes it is enough.

RELATED READINGS

Berger, Peter. (1963). *Invitation to Sociology*. New York: Anchor Doubleday.

Krause, Elliot. (1980). *Why Study Sociology?* New York: Random House.

Lee, Alfred McClung. (1978). *Sociology for Whom?* New York: Oxford University Press.

Mills, C. Wright. (1959). *The Sociological Imagination*. New York: Oxford University Press.

Nhat Hanh, Thich. (1975). *The Miracle of Mindfulness*. Boston: Beacon Press.

CHAPTER TWO

The Social World
As a Human Invention

A dollar bill is just a piece of paper. Although it is nicely printed, it is not a precious work of art. So how can a dollar bill have value? Why should anyone trade a cup of coffee for a piece of paper? It can only be because people with coffee believe that paper money can be traded for things they want. If people did not believe that paper money could be traded for things they want, such money would be worthless.

The power and reality of money derive from shared belief, nothing more. People who have lots of money are powerful because they can use their money to get others to work for them. If no one would trade goods and services for money, having money would bring a person no power. For money to bring power, people must create and share a belief in its value—and then they must act as if that belief were true.

Think of the diplomas you have or will get. You probably hope that these pieces of paper will help you get a job. But why should anyone give you a job because of a piece of paper? A diploma is no proof that you are competent, honest, or hard-working. If a diploma helps you get a job, it is only because an employer believes that in getting the diploma you acquired skills and habits that will make you a good worker. If employers stopped believing this, diplomas would be worthless in the labor market, and many schools would be empty.

Wars could not happen without shared belief. If a teacher said to you, "The students in the back row are evil and you must kill them before they kill you," you would probably not rise up and attack anybody. But suppose the president went on television and said, "The people in Oceania are evil and want to destroy our way of life, so we must bomb them before they attack us." What then? Would you volunteer to fly the planes and drop bombs? Would you cheer as the bombs fell? Many people would, even though they knew nothing about the people in Oceania.

For wars to happen, people in one country must believe that ordinary people in another country are a serious threat; that politicians tell the truth; that it is okay to kill if an elected official says so; and that there is no peaceful way to resolve conflict. When these beliefs are plainly stated, they seem so unlikely to be true that it is astounding that wars ever occur. Yet wars involving millions of people have occurred and still do. We can see from this that shared belief is enormously consequential.

To talk about the power of shared belief is to talk about the power of ideas. In America, where many people like to think of themselves as down-to-earth, the power of ideas is often not grasped. Sociological mindfulness helps us appreciate this power more fully. As the examples of money, diplomas, and wars show, ideas matter a great deal. (When a person says, "Ideas are just talk; they don't matter," s/he is misled by a dangerous idea.) But we should also see that money, diplomas, and wars are not special cases. Every part of the social world exists only because of the ideas people embrace and act upon.

What the Social World Is Made Of

To say that the social world exists only *because of* ideas does not mean that it is an illusion. Bodies are not illusions, nor are their tendencies to act in certain ways. Families, schools, banks, churches, clubs, corporations, towns, governments, armies, and nations are not illusions, either. You cannot wish them away. They consist of people doing things together in recurrent orderly ways. That is really what the social world is made of: patterns of activity.

We don't usually put it that way. Usually we talk about families, schools, banks, churches, clubs, corporations, towns, governments, armies, nations, and so on. But these are just names for patterns of activity that involve lots of people. It is because people share ideas about how to do things together that these patterns persist.

Ideas let us get things done together, in familiar ways, day after day. Without ideas to guide, inspire, and justify what we do, we would have no society. Ideas do not grow on trees, of course; we cannot just pick one to help when we are confused, disorganized, or in conflict with others. If we lack the ideas we need to solve certain problems, or to inspire or justify certain actions, then we must create those ideas. Humans have a wonderful, and sometimes frightening, capacity for doing this. We can interpret, imagine, or justify almost anything.

The social world is no less real because its existence depends on ideas invented by human beings. Its reality is different, however, from that of stars and trees and bacteria. Humans did not create stars and trees and bacteria, all of which existed long before hominids evolved on earth. On the other hand, there were no families, schools, churches, governments, and so on until humans came along. These things exist only because of ideas and ways of doing things devised, ages ago, by human beings struggling to survive.

To say that the social world is a human invention sounds strange because this makes it seem arbitrary and flimsy, and that is not how we usually perceive it. The social world usually seems solid and durable, as if it existed apart from us and could be touched. It also seems compelling and real, at least most of the time.

One reason the social world is durable is that people refuse to doubt the ideas that hold it together. Suppose, for example, that you thought your parents were alien shape shifters. If you told anyone of your belief, you would seem crazy. People wouldn't believe you, because to do so they would have to doubt many of the ideas on which their sense of reality depends. Most people, even those who act crazy at times, dislike this kind of disorientation. Every human mind strains in the opposite direction—toward making sense.

People also hold tightly to ideas because those ideas tell them what is right and wrong. "Thou shalt not kill" is just an idea, but it is a good one for guiding behavior, since it makes it safe to live with others. To threaten such a basic idea is to threaten society itself. There are many other such ideas about moral behavior, ideas that people see as essential to hold society (as they would like it to be) together. It is no wonder that people resist changing these ideas and even insist that such ideas be respected as sacred.

Ideas like this also allow people to feel good about themselves. How do you know that you are a good person? Because you have learned a set of ideas for judging yourself and your behavior. You have probably learned, for example, that kindness, generosity, and forgiveness are qualities of a good person. If you see these qualities in yourself, you can feel worthy of esteem in your own eyes and in the eyes of others. All of us relish these feelings of self-worth and resist changing the ideas on which such feelings depend.

The ideas that hold society together or help people feel good about themselves are often protected by other ideas. For example, some people might say, "These principles on which our society is based come from God and must never be changed." Other people might say, "In ancient times our wisest elders devised these principles, and we must not change them or else our society and everything we hold dear will perish." In either case, the attempt is to make society durable. To the people in it, a society thus will seem solid and real, for as long as it lasts.

Ideas shape people's feelings, too. When people settle into a way of understanding the world, they are also settling into a way of feeling about it, about others, and about themselves. Perhaps these feelings are pleasant, perhaps not. Either way, people can feel as if they are being pushed around emotionally—perhaps pushed toward feelings they don't want to have—when their ideas are challenged. So it is no wonder that people resist giving up familiar ideas and try to keep the world as they know it intact.

Habits and Invisible Ideas

You might wonder where all these familiar ideas can be found. Are they in books? Some are. But most exist only in people's heads, or are embodied in habit, and have never been spoken or written down. None of us is aware of all the ideas we hold and act upon. This is because many of our ideas are deep assumptions so taken for granted that, under ordinary circumstances, we do not think to question them.

You probably assume, for example, that this book is not a radio transmitter beaming messages into your brain. You probably do not suspect that the paper is coated with a drug, absorbed through the skin, that causes ringing in the ears. You probably also assume that this book will not explode when you reach page 67. Yet you have not been conscious of making any such assumptions, because they were so deep that you never became aware of them. A lot of our behavior is like this, rooted in places we never look.

The invisibility of the ideas that hold the social world together is part of what makes it seem so real. It's as if the social world were held together by invisible threads that wrap around us. Only when we try to pull away, to break from the pattern in some way, do we experience the realness, the tangible force, of the threads. If we are sociologically mindful we can see these threads being spun by ordinary people in everyday life.

Many of the ideas that hold the social world together are invisible because they are built into habit. For example, as a child you were probably taught to brush your teeth before bed. Perhaps you asked why and your parents explained about cavities and dentists. You still know all this, but now you brush your teeth as a matter of habit. The idea "I should brush my teeth to avoid painful dental work" is built into your habit; you don't have to review the ideas that originally led to the formation of the habit. This is true of all habits. Once upon a time we were told why we should do a certain thing, or maybe we figured it out for ourselves, and now we do it without thinking. The guiding ideas are still there, though visible only as habits.

Teeth-brushing is a dull example, but it makes a useful point: some seemingly personal habits are part of a culture. Before you were born, someone devised teeth-brushing as a way to avoid tooth decay. This was a solution (or a partial one) to a problem that existed before you did. Today almost all children are taught to brush their teeth. This is the sense in which teeth-brushing has become part of the culture. People now do it routinely.

Culture is created in this way. Someone finds a solution to a problem, other people see that it works and adopt it, and eventually the solution becomes "what everyone does." For a time people remember the idea behind the practice, but then, after a while, they forget. "This is just how we do things," they begin to say. When children come along they are taught the practice as a matter of course, perhaps with little explanation of the ideas on which it was originally based. It is as if the practice—the behavior that solves the problem— becomes part of a sediment that constitutes culture.

One time a student talked in class about her career plans. She expected to work hard after graduation, get promoted fast, and make lots of money. Then she said she would slow down when it came time to have babies. I asked her why, if she wanted to pursue a career with such zeal, she would impede her upward climb by having babies. She looked at me and didn't say anything for a moment. Then she said, "I don't know. I guess I never considered *not* getting married and having babies." Now there is a powerful cultural habit. It is so ingrained that many people do not even think about behaving differently.

Confronting the Social World As Ready-Made

Think about your first experience of school. There you found a set of arrangements worked out before you arrived. No one asked if you liked having teachers, principals, and other students around; no one asked if you liked homework, tests, and grades; no one asked if you liked meeting indoors, sitting in hard desks, and having only a half hour for recess. All this—the social world of school—was there waiting for you, and you had to deal with it, like it or not. What you were facing were other people's habitual ways of doing things together.

When you take a new job it is much the same. Your boss says, "This is how we do things here. This is what your job consists of." Your coworkers say, "You can bend the rules a little, but not too much." Again you face a set of arrangements and must adjust to a reality that seems to exist apart from you. We go through life like this, repeatedly adjusting to habits and expectations formed by people who preceded us. Experiencing this time and again makes the social world seem very real—and of course it is, as long as everyone carries on as if it is.

The social world seems so real in part because it confronts us as ready-made. As children, we're taught the ideas and habits that our parents and teachers found useful. We don't have much choice about this. Although we might question some of what we're taught, we mostly accept it because it's hard to get along otherwise.

Every society is built on a set of practices through which people meet their needs for food, clothing (usually), and shelter. To change these practices—especially those that seem to work well—is risky. People are reluctant to abandon an old but workable system and thereby risk being unable to provide for themselves. Those who benefit the most from the old system will of course be least likely to want to change it. Anyone who tries to do so may discover that the social world is maintained not only with ideas that affect minds, but also with tools, such as guns and bullets, that affect bodies.

Making People Disappear

It is not easy to become and remain mindful of the social world as humanly-made. For many reasons the social world seems to be "just there," as if no one were responsible for making it. So what? What difference does it make if we forget that the social world is a human invention? The difference it makes is like that between using one's tools with an awareness of what they are good for and letting those tools—as if they had minds and will of their own—take charge.

The failure to see the social world as humanly-made is called reification, which can also be defined as the tendency to see the humanly-made world as having a will and force of its own, apart from human beings. For example, someone might say, "Computer technology is the major force behind changes in our economy today." In this statement, computer technology is reified because it is spoken of as having a will of its own, independent of human beings. It is technology that appears to make things happen.

"Computer technology," however, is only metal and plastic. People forge these materials, turn them into computers and other devices, and then decide how to put such tools to work. All along the way there are people who choose what to build and how to use the results. But if we talk about technology as if it were a force in its own right, the people who do the building and choosing disappear. It thus seems as if technology is like gravity or the wind—a natural force about which we can do nothing.

Reification keeps us from seeing that the force attributed to technology comes from *people* choosing to do things together in certain ways. If we don't see this, we may forget to ask important questions, such as, Who is choosing to build what kinds of devices? Why? How will our society be changed? Who stands to benefit and who stands to lose because of these changes? Should we avoid these changes? Who will be held accountable if these changes hurt people? Should we decide to use technology in some other ways?

Here is another example of reification: "The market responded with enthusiasm to today's rise in interest rates, although economists predict that this could have unfavorable consequences for employment." You've probably heard this kind of statement before. It sounds like a report about a flood or some other natural disaster. Yet a market is just a lot of people doing things together in a certain way; interest rates are established by people; and employment results from choices by employers. Reification makes these people and their choices disappear.

In a large complex society the tendency to reify is strong because it can be hard to see where, how, and by whom decisions are made. And so it is easier to say that technology, the market, or a mysterious *They* is making things happen. Even people who ought to know better get caught up in this. When sociologists say things like, "Trends in inner-city industrial development are causing changes in family structure," they too are guilty of reification. Such language again makes it seem as if no one is responsible for choosing to act in a way that hurts or helps others.

Reification thus keeps us from seeing who is doing what to whom, and how, such that certain consequences arise. This makes it hard to hold anyone accountable for the good or bad results arising from their actions. Usually it is powerful people whose actions are hidden and who get off the hook.

Reification can also make us feel powerless because the social world comes to seem like a place that is beyond human control. If we attribute independent force to abstractions such as "technology," "the market," "government," "trends," "social structure," or "society," then it can seem pointless even to try to intervene and make things happen differently. We might as well try to stop the tides. People who think this way are likely to remain passive even when they see others being put out of work, living in poverty, or caught up in war, because they will feel that nothing can be done.

When we reify the social world we are confusing its reality with that of stars and trees and bacteria. These things indeed exist (as material entities) independent of human ideas and action. But no part of the social world does. To reify is to forget this; it is to forget to be mindful of the social world as a humanly-made place. As a result, we forget that it is within our collective power to re-create the world in a better way. If we are sociologically mindful, we recognize that the social world as it now exists is just one of many possibilities.

Inventing Categories and Inventing People

Even if we believe that one way of schooling, churching, or governing is best, we can still admit that these ways of doing things together depend on ideas and habits invented by people. It can be harder to accept that the same principle applies to social constructions that have to do with who we think we are.

For example, many people think that they belong to a "race" and that races are visible, biological realities. But races, too, are human inventions. When people talk about distinct races, as if there were significant genetic differences among human groups that produce differences in intelligence and behavior, they are mistaken. "White" people, "black" people, and so on had to be defined into existence. Such groups were invented, once upon a time, largely for political reasons.

Race is, of course, a social reality. Based on skin tone and place of ancestral origin, people are defined as belonging to races, and such labels can affect how people are treated, whom they live with, the customs they learn, and how they think of themselves. But again, all this results from the invention of schemes for sorting people into groups. We could sort people according to eye color, height, or warmth of heart. If we acted on these new schemes, they would be just as real and consequential as our current ideas about race.

Just as some people think they can see race when they see a person's skin, others think they can see gender when they see an infant's genitals. "Ah, this one has a penis—it's a boy. And this one, with a vagina, is a girl," people say. But it is a mistake to equate genitalia with gender. While penises and vaginas are plainly part of human bodies, gender is something that humans must be taught.

If we did not assign the meanings we do to penises and vaginas, if we did not have the cultural habits of treating the possessors of these organs differently, we would not produce girls and boys, women and men. Such creatures are the results of many people embracing and acting on similar ideas. Other ideas and behaviors would produce different kinds of people. Men and women, as we know them, are just one set of possibilities.

Seeing race and gender as social constructions can be troubling because it makes it seem as if we have no substance as individuals, as if our sense of who we are could melt into air at any time. There is a grain of truth in this fear, even though people do not dissolve so easily.

It is true that if you had been born into a different social world, you would be a different person. You might never have learned to think of yourself as, for example, a man or a woman, as black or white, as European or African, as gay or straight. All these identities derive from invented categories; they are not part of nature. In fact, all your ideas about who and what you are come from the social world in which you were raised.

Perhaps you can see here another reason why a humanly-made world seems so real: It gets inside us. The ideas that hold the social world together tell us who we are. If we didn't keep believing in the reality of the social world, we might lose a sense of our realness as individuals. Fearing such a condition, many people refuse to study the making of the social world, preferring instead to believe that it has supernatural origins and follows a blueprint devised in the heavens.

Inventing the Truth

If any of my ideas run counter to ones you hold, you might wonder whose are true, mine or yours. That's an important matter to consider, but I will let you do it on your own. Here I want to make another point about the constructedness of the social world. The point is this: The rules we use to decide which ideas are true are also invented.

You could, for example, follow a rule that says, "Accept as true what is written in books that are widely believed to be divinely inspired." Or you could follow a rule that says, "Accept as true only those things you can verify for yourself." Or your rule could be "Accept as true only what has been proven by science." You can find people who embrace these and other rules for deciding what is true.

Whichever rule you prefer, it will be one that you learned as a matter of growing up in a particular place and time. It will be a rule invented by people and passed on to you like any other notion about how best to do things. Figuring out what is real and true is as much a matter of cultural habit as teeth-brushing. We can do it almost without thinking, which is helpful in some cases and harmful in others.

This is how it is with humans: First we make rules for believing, then we follow our rules as a matter of habit, settle our beliefs, and presume to know how things really are, as if the truth had come to us through no effort at all. It might seem self-evident, for example, that the moon is not made of green cheese. To accept this claim as true, however, we must share understandings of what is meant by "moon," "cheese," and "is made of." We must also agree on what would constitute evidence for or against such a claim (must we have a sample of the moon? what if the sample is 99% mineral and 1% cheese?). If we can agree on these matters, we can create a true idea about the moon, just like we create true ideas about other things.

If we practice sociological mindfulness, we pay attention not only to how the world is socially constructed, but also to how we invent ways to decide what is real and true. If we do this, we may be more open to understanding how other people arrive at different ideas about what is real and true. We might also be less likely to insist that other people accept our picture of the world as the only true picture. We might even be more open to considering the pictures other people create.

The point of being mindful about the invention of truth is not to discover the best rules for deciding what is true. There are no best rules, only rules that are more or less useful, depending on our purposes. So the point is not to get at truer truths, but to better understand how social reality is created by paying attention to how people decide what is real and true. You will see two things if you pay attention to this process: Not everyone has an equal say in deciding what is real and true, and truth often bends toward power.

How to See the Social World Being Made

How can we see the social world being made? All we need to do is to pay attention in the right way to what is going on around us all the time. Instructions for how to pay attention to the social construction of the world can be put in the form of admonitions and questions. It is a matter of knowing what to look for and what to ask.

First, look for people solving problems together. Here you will see habits and routines being formed. When two or more people confront a common problem, arrive at a similar view of it, and devise a solution for it, they are creating a piece of social reality. When their solution is taught to other people, and when that way of doing things becomes a matter of habit for them, a piece of culture is formed. If this routine way of doing things involves lots of people coordinating their actions day after day, an institution is formed.

Ask who benefits from certain ways of doing things. Solutions for some people can create problems for others. For example, putting people out of work ("downsizing" a firm) might increase profits for employers, but it hurts workers. Certain ways of organizing school might be good for teachers because students are kept under control, but this might not be so good for students. So in looking at any social arrangement ask, Who benefits and who suffers? You will find that there is often a great deal of conflict underlying the construction of the social world.

Watch for the invention of labels and categories, especially ones applied to people. Pay attention to disputes over the meanings given to these labels and categories, which often become the basis for people's identities. Observe how people are put into one category or another, how they are labeled in one way or another, and how they come to accept or reject certain identities. The meanings given to these labels, categories, and identities determine whether people will be respected, ignored, or abused. If you watch as these meanings are created and negotiated, you'll see social reality being constructed and people's lives being shaped.

Be mindful of the labels and categories you use to know yourself and others. Ask who invented these labels and categories. Ask who benefits from them and who is hurt. Ask how the meanings of these labels and categories affect people's behavior. The answers will not always be easy to find, but they must be sought if you want to be a responsible participant in the making of social reality. How else can you understand what you are doing and what you are a part of?

Watch for the assumptions people make when they claim that something in the social world is real. Look to see what people take for granted. Look to see what they refuse to doubt. Look for these things and you'll find the bedrock on which people build their sense of reality. It is good practice to inspect your own foundations as well.

Also pay attention to how people create among themselves a version of the truth. To see this you have to watch what goes on between people when matters of truth are being decided. Who says what? What sorts of arguments are accepted as plausible and convincing? What kinds of evidence are accepted as compelling? What assumptions are rejected right from the start? If you can discern these things, if you can learn to see the process as it unfolds, you will be able to see how groups of people create the different truths and social worlds in which they live.

Remaking the Social World

Although I have said that the social world seems to exist as if it were a hard and durable thing that could survive on its own, that is only how it seems. In fact, the social world could not continue to exist if we did not reenact it every day. We are part of it; our thoughts, feelings, and behaviors keep it going. Part of being sociologically mindful is paying attention to how we do this. Which ideas do we pass on to others, perhaps inadvertently? Which habits, routines, and institutions do we support with our actions? Which ones do we oppose? If we are to understand the making of the social world, we have to see how we contribute to its making.

Part of being sociologically mindful of the constructedness of the social world is seeing the possibility of changing it. This means recognizing the possibility of acting differently, of choosing not to support arrangements that are harmful or unjust. The consequences of not conforming might be severe, but we should not pretend that we do not have a choice. The only time we really do not have a choice is when it never occurs to us that we do. Once we are aware of the possibility of acting differently, it is dishonest to say, "I had no choice. I had to do what I had to do." What this really means is, "Because the consequences of doing X were more than I could bear, I chose to do Y instead." It is harder to say this, because it means taking responsibility for what we do.

What we do as individuals might not seem to have much effect on the world. Often our acts of resistance seem to go unnoticed. But it is through small acts that the world is remade.

Suppose you realize that a certain cultural habit (e.g., throwing away usable glass bottles) harms the environment. That is a problem for you, so you find a way around it, a way to act differently. You offer that solution (a way to recycle) to others who share your concern.

Pretty soon quite a few people are acting differently, and the social world is being changed, if only gradually and in a small way. Perhaps at some point a balance is tipped and more dramatic changes occur suddenly. History unfolds like this sometimes.

The making of the social world is always a collaboration; we can neither make nor remake anything *social* by ourselves. Our ideas, our "solutions," must be communicated to and must appeal to other people. Only by paying attention to others' unmet needs and showing them how to do things differently so that these needs can be met are we likely to make any big changes. Our power lies, in other words, in our ability to communicate with others, through words and deeds, so that they can see the benefits of doing things differently.

It might seem as if there is a contradiction here. On the one hand, I have said that everything about the social world is a result of shared belief and of people doing things together in recurrent orderly ways. This seems to leave little room for individuality. Yet in talking about world-making and change, I have emphasized individual responsibility and initiative. How can it be both ways? If people must adjust themselves to established cultural habits and other social arrangements, if they are so thoroughly shaped by these habits and arrangements, how can they ever resist?

For one thing, human minds are unruly. They are not like computers that do only what they're told. Minds generate images and longings and strange, unpredictable impulses. These products of mind are the seeds of dissatisfaction, resistance, creativity, and change. No doubt you can conjure images of desirable objects, situations, and experiences—ones that do not exist in your life today. Your mind can always reach beyond everyday life and create longings for something more— more pleasures, challenges, satisfactions—than you now enjoy. Your mind, and everyone else's, tends to generate dissatisfaction with what exists, if only because you can imagine things being better.

When people share their feelings about what exists, and share their imaginings about what might exist, they often begin to recognize problems where they saw none before, perhaps because of what they took for granted. This sort of conversation can create awareness that a problem is in fact widely shared, even if no one had seen it very clearly before. If people then say, "Let's see if we can solve our common problem," and go on to devise a new way of doing things together, the social world is indeed remade.

So while it is true that for the most part we must adjust to the social world that precedes us, even as we learn to adjust—in part by developing minds and the ability to get along with others—we also acquire the inclination and power to remake the world, to force it to adjust to us, if only a little at a time. Being sociologically mindful, we thus see that human beings are both social products and social forces. Though we are shaped by the world, we are still, each of us, a place on earth where ideas and feelings clash inside a body that can act to affect other bodies. And that is how change is made to happen.

A student once said, "Seeing the world as humanly invented takes all the magic and mystery out of it, like the whole thing is nothing special." To him the world could be mysterious and special only if supernatural powers were behind it. I said that I wondered why some people needed to believe in the supernatural. I said that I marveled at the human capacity to invent ideas about such things. I said that it was a mystery to me how people, in a scientific era, could sustain belief in gods and ghosts. My point was to say that the social world becomes fascinating in new ways if we pay attention to its making, especially to the ironies and contradictions in which people entangle themselves.

We can be intensely mindful of how the social world is made and still not see all there is to see. There is always something new around the corner, behind our backs, or under our feet. And often we are so busy living that we don't see what we're making happen. This means that we can always spend tomorrow trying to understand what we did today. There is always more analytic thinking to be done about social life, since life always runs ahead of our ability to make sense of it.

Being sociologically mindful is thus not a way to see everything, as if everything could be so easily seen. It is a way to see more deeply into the process of world-making and to appreciate the nature of the social world as a human accomplishment. Even if we never fathom it fully, by trying to do so we can live more interesting and responsible lives. We can also see better how we might remake the world into a place where more people can live good lives.

RELATED READINGS

Becker, Howard S. (1986). *Doing Things Together*. Evanston, IL: Northwestern University Press.

Berger, Peter, & Luckmann, Thomas. (1966). *The Social Construction of Reality*. Garden City, NY: Doubleday.

Douglas, Jack. (1970). *Understanding Everyday Life*. Chicago: Aldine.

Lorber, Judith. (1993). *Paradoxes of Gender*. New Haven, CT: Yale University Press.

Omi, Michael, & Winant, Howard. (1994). *Racial Formation in the United States* (2nd ed.). New York: Routledge.

Schutz, Alfred. (1932/1967). *The Phenomenology of the Social World*. Evanston, IL: Northwestern University Press.

CHAPTER THREE

Seeing Connections

One time a student said, "I believe in tradition and think that in the home the man should be dominant." Earlier this student had said that she wanted to be a corporate attorney, so I asked if she expected to be treated as an equal at work. "Absolutely," she said. Then I asked, "Do you think it might be hard for men to see you as an equal at work if they are used to treating women as subordinates at home?" She looked puzzled, but another student saw my point and said to her, "Think about your husband. If he's used to you being subordinate at home, that's what he's going to expect from the women he works with." Another student said, "If you raise boys in a home where a man is dominant, they'll expect to be dominant themselves when they go out into the world, and that's going to hurt other women." Another student tried to sum it up: "If women settle for inequality at home, they're never going to get equality in work or politics."

Part of being sociologically mindful is seeing how our actions in one part of life are the causes and consequences of what happens elsewhere. In the example above, the first student didn't see how accepting inequality at home could keep her and other women from achieving equality at work. She was not sufficiently aware of how home life and work life are connected, such that her actions in one realm could produce unintended consequences in the other.

Here is another example. For various reasons, some people don't want to pay taxes to support programs that help the poor. And so they vote for politicians who say they will lower taxes by cutting spending on welfare, education, public housing, and school-lunch programs. You might or might not think that cutting aid to the poor is a mean and selfish policy. But without judging it in those terms, we can ask whether it is mindful or not.

The first thing we should note is that the Federal Reserve Board sets interest rates so that unemployment stays, according to official figures, at about 5 percent (it is really about twice as high). This means that there will be millions of people without jobs, through no fault of their own. If there are not enough jobs to go around, and public aid is eliminated, what is the result likely to be? Probably more crime, illness, and despair—all of which have costs: higher taxes to pay for more police and prisons; higher rates for health insurance to cover the cost of emergency-room care for the poor; higher rates for insurance to cover the costs of more burglaries; greater resentment and fear between the poor and the middle class. So where is the savings? Because of how our society works, there would probably be no savings, and in many ways there would be higher costs and more suffering for everyone, except the very rich.

Sociological mindfulness does not tell us how to make tax policy. But if we pay attention to how different parts of society are connected, we are less likely to make wasteful and destructive choices about how to collect and use our common wealth. Being sociologically mindful, we can see that when we pay less for one kind of thing, we might be creating conditions that will force us, eventually, to pay more for another.

Sociological mindfulness means taking a larger view of things. For example, in the case of taxes and public aid, it would be wise to look at how much of our federal budget is spent on Aid to Families with Dependent Children, which is commonly known as welfare (less than 2%) and how much is spent on the military (30–50%, depending on what is counted as military). We might thus see that there is plenty of wealth to provide food, housing, education, health care, and so on to all who need it—if only we did not spend billions of dollars a year to build weapons.

While it is sometimes helpful to study one problem at a time, it is also important to see how problems are connected. Consider the example of failure in school. Why do so many children and teenagers do poorly in school or drop out? Only part of an answer can be found by looking at what happens inside schools. To understand why students do badly in school, we must look at how schools are connected to the larger society.

Students who are hungry or tired probably will not do well in school. Why are they hungry or tired? Perhaps because their families can't afford adequate food and quiet housing. And why is this? Perhaps because there aren't enough good jobs to go around. And why is this? Perhaps because employers want a high rate of unemployment to keep wages down and profits up. A lack of jobs can also dampen motivation. If school is boring and doesn't seem likely to result in a job, why stay? To make another connection, school might be boring because teachers are underpaid, overworked, and worn out. Why is this? Perhaps because so much money is spent on machines for killing, instead of on education.

The problem of failure in school is more complicated than I have made it out to be. But that is precisely the point: The problem is complicated because it arises out of a web of connections between schools, students, teachers, families, corporations, and government. To understand the problem, in a complete way, we must trace out these connections. Simply attributing the problem to something inside schools or, as some do, to a deficiency inside students, is not very helpful. The point of tracing out connections is to find the roots of whatever problem we are trying to understand and solve.

Consider again the link between equality at work and equality in the home. Women cannot compete as men's equals at work if they are doing a second shift of cleaning, laundry, and childcare at home. A man whose wife does these chores for him, or a man who doesn't do his share, is freer to devote himself to a job. As this freedom translates into higher earnings, a man expects and gains more power in the home because his job becomes the chief source of family income. The connection now runs two ways: A little extra power at home, arising out of old ideas about gender, can give a man an edge at work, which can in turn, over time, amplify his power in the home. Seeing things in this way implies that to reduce inequality between women and men we must tackle inequalities in different but deeply connected realms of life.

Awareness of Unintended Consequences

Perhaps you are thinking, "The household inequality problem is not so complicated. If two people are busy pursuing their careers and are doing well, they can hire a maid." This is a good example of a solution that is not a solution, as we can see if we are mindful of how unintended consequences can come about. To see these consequences we must first see connections.

There is clearly a connection between a couple's income and the act of hiring a maid. Only people who have high incomes can afford to do this. There is also a connection between the lack of job opportunities and the availability of maids. If there were lots of jobs offering good pay and working conditions, few people would choose to clean others' toilets for a living. These are obvious connections; others are harder to see.

To see these connections we must note first that most maids are women, and, second, that when a couple hires a maid, it is usually because the woman in the couple has decided she does not want to do so much housework. This situation typically arises, as suggested earlier, because the man in the couple resists doing a fair share of the work. If he did his share, chances are that a maid would not be needed.

So what is going on here? Is any real change being made? Not much. There is no challenge to the idea that housework is primarily a woman's responsibility. It is just a different woman who ends up doing the work. The couple simply uses some of its income to put the burden of inequality on the back of a poorer woman. The result may be a little more equality in housework within the couple, but inequality in society as a whole is reinforced. This is doubly true if the couple is white and the maid is not.

The situation is not much different if the housecleaner is a man. In this case the idea that housework is a woman's responsibility is less obviously reinforced (though it is still typically the woman in a couple who hires a housecleaner). But what is still reinforced is the idea that inequality is okay. Once again a person with few job opportunities cleans the toilets of others, who are then freer to do more enriching things. The message conveyed by such an arrangement is this: "I am too busy making money and having fun to be bothered with cleaning up my own messes. Other people, those who have less money, should do that work for me."

We can see here a connection to a set of ideas that make inequality seem acceptable. One such idea is that a person with money is entitled to have others do his or her dirty work. To use such an idea, if only implicitly, to justify hiring a housecleaner affirms the rightness of inequality. It is as if to say, "Wealth determines human worth, and it is thus okay for a person of my wealth and worth to hire a person of lesser worth to clean up after me." Parents who hire a housecleaner teach this principle to their children, who learn that people who are rich enough do not have to take responsibility for cleaning up the messes they make.

Men can use these same ideas to argue that they should be free from doing dirty work and have more time for "serious" work, and for play, because, after all, they make more money and are thus worth more than others, usually women, who earn less. The connection here is between the perpetuation of two seemingly different kinds of inequality, one having to do with economics, the other with gender. Both kinds of inequality are connected because a similar belief—about what determines the relative worth of human beings—underlies and supports them.

Sociological mindfulness brings these connections to light. What we are trying to see is how our actions, and the ideas we use to justify them, can have intended and unintended consequences because of how the social world works. If our society were not so fraught with inequalities, the meaning and consequences of hiring a housecleaner might be different.

Analyzing Moral Problems

The need to be mindful of connections increases when the problem at hand evokes strong feelings. Abortion is a good example. To see the point I will try to make about sociological mindfulness, it will help if you can set aside, for a time, your feelings about this issue. Try to shift into an analytic frame of mind.

Opponents of abortion believe that a fetus is an unborn child and that abortion is akin to murder. Others believe that until a fetus can survive outside the womb, it is part of a woman's body. In this view, abortion is the exercise of a woman's right to dominion over her body and her life. A point that is often missed is that abortion is not just about the rights of individual women to control their bodies. If we are mindful of how our society works, we can see that there is more at stake: Restricting abortion makes it unlikely that women will ever achieve equality with men.

If women are forced to be mothers, they cannot compete as equals with men who need never worry that pregnancy, or the obligation to care for a child, will impede their striving for success in work and politics. A lack of freedom to decide whether to give birth and care for children puts women at a disadvantage. Forcing women to be mothers by restricting abortion also reinforces the idea that being a mother is a woman's most important role, implying that it is best if women make babies and homes rather than laws or economic policy.

There is another connection to see here. If women cannot get safe, legal abortions, they will get them under unsafe conditions, risking injury and death. This has always been the case when abortion is restricted. What this means is that not only women's wishes, but their safety, are ignored when abortion is restricted. Such a policy thus conveys messages about women's role and worth. It says, in effect, that women should not resist motherhood and that women are less important to society than the fetuses they carry.

Denying women the option of ending a pregnancy is connected to inequality in another way. A policy of restricting abortion implies that women are incapable of making wise choices in these personal matters of life and death. If that is so, then women are surely incapable of dealing with the larger matters of life and death that concern men, matters such as whether to wage wars and kill millions of fully grown people. Restricting abortion thus not only impedes women's ability to compete with men; it also reinforces the idea that women are not men's moral and intellectual equals when it comes to dealing with the vital affairs of society.

Perhaps this sounds like an argument for abortion. Not necessarily. It is an attempt to practice sociological mindfulness with regard to the abortion issue, so as to see more of what is at stake. This way of seeing does not inevitably lead to the conclusion that abortion is right. You might believe, for example, that abortion is an undesirable practice because it reinforces a view of inconvenient life as disposable and that such an attitude will have harmful consequences in the long run.

Differences in values may also lead to different conclusions. You might believe, for example, that a zygote or a fetus deserves no less moral consideration than a fully grown woman and that restricting women's freedom is a reasonable price to pay for protecting a fetus's "right to life." If so, then you may think it is fine to restrict or outlaw abortion. But to arrive at any sound and responsible conclusions either way, one must be mindful of the connections between abortion and women's freedom and equality.

Sociological mindfulness can help us see more of what must be taken into account in seeking solutions to moral problems. This is mostly a matter of trying to see connections between our acts and their consequences, in light of how the social world works. The example of abortion shows that being mindful in this way requires a willingness to look with some detachment at how the social world works, whether we like it or not. This does not mean ignoring our hearts when making moral judgments. It means also using our heads.

Everywhere a Sign, Every Sign a Doorway

The social world is full of signs called indexes. Like all signs, indexes point to, refer to, or represent something else. Learning to see and read indexes is part of learning to be sociologically mindful. To read or interpret an index sociologically is to see its connection to some aspect of how the social world works.

Imagine, for example, an unpaved road in an area where many poor people live. The road is an index. It points to the poverty and powerlessness of the people who live nearby. That is an interpretation, of course; we would want to check to see if it was true. But it is a plausible interpretation, given how our society works. We know that people usually like to have nice, paved roads and that officials who control road-building are usually more responsive to people who have money. The unpaved road could thus also be seen as an index of how government works in this country. If we know how to read it, the road can point us to many other things.

Some indexes attach to people. For example, we learn to read cars, clothes, and houses as indexes of a person's wealth. We learn to read behavior as an index of character. We can do this because we have ideas about how society works and why people act as they do. These ideas allow us to see connections between indexes and other conditions. In general, the more such ideas we possess, the more connections we can see. If people don't see the same connections, it is probably because they have different ideas about how the world works.

Sociological mindfulness does not tell us precisely how an index is connected to some other condition. Nor does it tell us what is an index of what. Being sociologically mindful simply means trying to see how conditions, customs, and events might be signs that point to other things. We can do this by making a habit of asking, "What does this condition, custom, or event *mean?* What other realities does it *point to?* What does it *say* about the nature of our society?" The answers we arrive at depend on our knowledge of how the world works.

Non-Obvious Indexes

Most people learn to read the behavior, appearance, and possessions of individuals as indexes to their character and wealth. This is a basic interpretive skill. But sociological mindfulness can take us further. Things that once didn't seem meaningful are examined more closely and probed for their meaning. In this sense, sociological mindfulness amplifies our powers of interpretation.

Here are examples of arrangements, customs, and conditions that can be read as indexes. My interpretations are based on my understanding of how the social world works. Your ideas about how the world works might be different. If so, some of my interpretations will seem strange. That's fine. You do not have to interpret a sign the same way I do to appreciate that it is a sign. What matters is forming the habit of seeing parts of the social world as indexes.

I have already mentioned the vast share of our common wealth that is spent on tools for killing and on training people to use these tools. You might think this situation is atrocious, merely unfortunate, or quite all right. For the moment it doesn't matter. I ask you just to think about what it means that we use so much of our common wealth to kill or prepare to kill other human beings. What does this say about our society? What does it say about us as a people?

I think it says that we live in a society where the rich and powerful use a large part of our common wealth to become richer and more powerful by creating well-equipped armies to control workers, gain access to raw materials, and keep trade markets open. It says that we live in a world where many people feel they have no choice but to violently resist oppression and exploitation. It says we live in a world where some people feel entitled to exploit others, as long as they have the power to do so. I think it also says that most of us are afraid to protest the use of our common wealth to create a huge apparatus of violence.

"Military spending" could be read differently. You might not agree that it points to what I think it does. Again, that is fine. What matters is not taking it for granted but instead seeing it as an indicator and a consequence of how our society works. Being sociologically mindful, we look at "military spending" as a doorway to other social realities. Once the door is opened, we can trace out connections and talk about what else they might lead us to see.

Here is another example. Today the conditions in many of our inner cities are wretched. Many industries have moved to more profitable locations. Good jobs are thus scarce and unemployment is high. Because so many people cannot find steady work, inner-city housing is deteriorating, drug use and street crime are rampant, rates of infant mortality are extremely high, schools are in bad shape, and good health care is hard to find. Many of the people living in these areas are members of racial minority groups.

In this case we could say that conditions in inner-city areas are indexes of how our economy works. When it is more profitable to move a factory elsewhere, that is what will be done, regardless of the effects on those who are left behind. But there is a different kind of index that appears in this situation. We can see it if we look beyond the cities themselves. Consider how most white Americans react to conditions in inner cities.

What is the reaction? The most visible reaction is to blame the poor, insist that they work harder, and cut off public aid. But the most widespread reaction among white Americans is disregard. The majority of white Americans are not demanding that more be done to help people in inner cities. Most white Americans seem to wish the problem would just go away.

What is the meaning of this lack of compassion? What does it say about white Americans? It can be read as an index of racism, although I think it points to more than that. It also points to white Americans' insecurity about their own economic status; to their desire to believe that their achievements are of their own doing; and to their feelings of powerlessness when it comes to solving problems that require generous use of our common wealth, over which we do not exercise democratic control. In this case the index is *action not taken*. If we are sociologically mindful, we can see that the *absence* of something can be a sign, too.

Social Organization As an Index

The ways we organize ourselves to accomplish tasks can also be read as indexes. In other words, our customary ways of doing things encode messages about us; they can be read as signs of what we value and what we fear. Consider, for example, our ways of schooling.

We give grades to individuals and insist that individuals do their own work. We separate school from home life, make teachers act as surrogate parents and bosses, break the school day into blocks of time, give students breaks and vacations, make students follow rules of order (raise your hand if you want to speak!), and punish students for violating these rules. What do these practices say about us? I think they say that we, or at least the people who organize schools, are mainly concerned with turning students into good workers.

Schooling does more than transmit knowledge and basic skills. Our *form* of schooling teaches students to be competitive individualists, to accept hierarchy and authority, to follow rules, and to get up every day and do meaningless work. Students who learn to accept this regimen adapt quickly to the world of work, which is organized in much the same way. If school were organized differently—with less hierarchy and authoritarian control, less regimentation and regulation by the clock, less competition, and more respect for students' real concerns—then students might not adapt so well to the demands of employers.

Do we really value creativity, independent moral judgment, and critical thinking as much as we say? The answer encoded in our form of schooling is "no." Even though some people, including many teachers, may value different kinds of knowledge, skills, and habits of mind than do employers, most schooling is organized to create good workers, rather than artists, social critics, and political activists. This fact can be seen as an index of the power of employers, and of business in general, to influence how we conduct seemingly non-economic activities in our society.

Let me suggest some other things that can be seen as indexes. You can try to read these on your own. Ask what they mean, what other realities they point to, and what they say about the nature of our society.

■ The popularity of violent movies and sports

■ The small percentage (1–3%) of chief executive officers of Fortune 500 firms who are women

■ The refusal of TV stations to run ads for condoms even in the midst of an AIDS epidemic

■ The intense interest many people have in the lives of actors and other celebrities

■ The format of television news programs

■ The continuing widespread belief in religion, even in a scientific age

■ The use of mood-altering drugs, such as alcohol and nicotine, by many middle-class people

■ The way in which political candidates "debate" and respond to each other during campaigns

■ The percentage (45%) of Americans who do not read books

You could see these items as mere curiosities and not give them another thought. Practicing sociological mindfulness, however, you can see them as doorways behind which lie interesting and complex connections to other aspects of the social world.

Connections to the Past

If you care to muse about the past, or about its connections to the present, you need not go to a museum. You are already in one. The past is congealed all around us. Our clothes, the language we speak, the houses we live in, the ideas we embrace, and the customs we practice are all bequeathed to us from the past. We do change these things, of course; but we do not start from scratch.

When we are sociologically mindful, we try to see how the past delivers us into the present moment, and what the present moment tells us about the past. We could call this "trying to see historical connections," or "looking backward to try to see how things today got to be what they are." It is like seeing things in the present as indexes to the past, although things in the present do not merely point to or refer to the past; they carry it with them.

This seems most obvious if we consider material objects, such as clothing and buildings. The clothes we wear and the ways we wear them are clearly matters of tradition. It is the same with our buildings and the ways we build them. Food is a good example, too—at every meal the past is served up to us. These solid objects seem to hold the past firmly in place. We can look at them and say, "This is how it was done long ago. And see? We are still doing it much the same way today." In these instances, evidence of the past is plain to see.

Knowledge itself is the past living in our minds and habits. We know what we know and do what we do—today—because of what others learned before us, thousands of years ago. This is evident right now, even as I am writing and you are (somewhat later) reading. Our language—each word, each grammatical rule—connects us not only to each other, but also to a common human past.

The idea that the present is connected to the past might seem obvious. Yet people often fail to see historical connections, sometimes because they don't want to. For example, many white people in the United States will say, "Racism is a problem of the past. Discrimination is illegal now. Everyone is on an equal footing. So we don't need affirmative action or special programs for racial minorities." Statements like these erase connections to the past—as if all the power and privileges white people accumulated while enslaving blacks for hundreds of years do not exist.

Here is another example. In the past, women gave up their family names upon getting married and took the last name of their new husband. This practice served to indicate that a woman, as a piece of property, had been transferred from one male (the father) to another (the new husband). Men did not change their names. Men were owners, not property.

Today we reject the idea of women as property, yet this name-changing practice persists. Why? Perhaps because many young women do not see the connection between this practice and the past. If so, they fail to see the significance of changing their names. They fail to see that giving up their names—when few men would consider doing such a thing—helps perpetuate the same idea on which an older form of patriarchy was based. The idea is that a woman's identity is determined by her relationship to a man. If we want to affirm the value and equality of women, it would seem wise to reject practices that keep an oppressive past alive in the present.

The example of name-changing suggests how to be sociologically mindful about connections between past and present. It is not enough to say, "The past shapes how we think and act today." That is an important recognition, but we must go further. Being sociologically mindful, we should ask, "How did this practice originate? What problems did it solve for whom?" Those questions can be answered only by looking into the past. To seek answers is not merely to satisfy curiosity about times gone by. It is to try to better understand what is going on now.

Deepening the Present

Being sociologically mindful of connections between past and present can also lead us to ask better questions about the present. For example, we can ask—about any traditional idea, custom, or social arrange-ment—"Does it serve the same purpose today as it did originally? Has it become dysfunctional in some way? If so, why has this tradition been preserved? Who benefits from carrying on this tradition—the same people as in the past? How has the tradition been changed over the years? Why?"

Asking these kinds of questions makes the present more complex and interesting. Finding answers can also help us to appreciate the constructedness of the social world. By looking at connections between the past and present, we see that what people intend to construct, once upon a time, can vary greatly from what comes about over time. Looking backward also helps us see how *contingency* (a peculiar mix of fateful circumstances) affects the making of the social world.

Earlier I used the example of slavery and the consolidation of political and economic power by whites. I said that this past shapes our present and that it is foolish and wrong to deny it. But there is still room for argument and for the weighing of evidence about exactly how this past shapes which parts of our present. Undertaking this kind of inquiry and conversation is part of being sociologically mindful.

Another way to be mindful of the past in the present involves listening to others here and now. Specifically, we should be mindful of the *meaning* of the past and the *feelings* these meanings evoke. The question is not whether people's ideas about the past are correct. Rather, the question is, "How do people's feelings about the past, whatever those feelings might be based on, affect how they behave in the present?"

Consider again the example of slavery. We might analyze how it has affected the balance of power between blacks and whites in the United States today. That is an important kind of analysis to do. But we must also consider the meaning of slavery as a part of our past. We must consider what this part of our past means to people today. We must take these meanings into account if we want to understand the present, because these meanings affect how blacks and whites get along. If my people were enslaved by yours for hundreds of years, and then you tell me, less than 150 years later, "Oh, that's no big deal, and it certainly doesn't have any bearing on the present," you can be sure that this will affect my feelings toward you.

Understanding how people define the past and how they feel about it is part of being sociologically mindful of connections between past and present. It is to see another way in which the past lives on inside us and affects what goes on between us. Here is one more example.

One time a few of us were talking about Atlanta, Georgia. We were all going to a conference there very soon. Everyone spoke well of the city. One person said, "It's amazing how they rebuilt the city after it burned in the Civil War." Another person in the group, a woman from Georgia, then said, "Honey, Atlanta didn't burn in the Civil War; it *was burned.*" She wanted to remind us that a horrible event didn't simply happen, but that a northern army had savaged a part of her home state. Her remark surprised me, since I had grown up in the North and had never met anyone with strong feelings about the Civil War. Our interaction on this occasion was affected by feelings arising from the meaning given to events that had happened over 120 years before.

We can argue about whether it is good or bad, useful or not, to hold onto certain parts of the past. But that is a different matter. The point here is that we can't deal well with others without being mindful of how the meanings they give to the past affect the meanings they give to things in the present. We must also be mindful of how people learn about the past and come to define it as they do. To know these things we must connect a person to his or her own past, as we must do with ourselves.

If we can't see these connections, the present will seem to just tumble into the future. The present itself might seem like a random configuration of circumstances. Practicing sociological mindfulness is a way to dispel this illusion and to find orderly connections between present and past. It is a way to avoid repeating mistakes of the past and to see when old dangers arise in new forms.

RELATED READINGS

Anderson, Elijah. (1990). *Streetwise: Race, Class, and Change in an Urban Community.* Chicago: University of Chicago Press.

Gottdiener, Mark. (1995). *Postmodern Semiotics: Material Culture and the Forms of Postmodern Life.* Cambridge, MA: Blackwell.

Kleinman, Sherryl. (1996). *Opposing Ambitions: Gender and Identity in an Alternative Organization.* Chicago: University of Chicago Press.

Schwalbe, Michael. (1996). *Unlocking the Iron Cage: The Men's Movement, Gender Politics, and American Culture.* New York: Oxford University Press.

Sennett, Richard, & Cobb, Jonathan. (1972). *The Hidden Injuries of Class.* New York: Vintage.

Snow, David, & Anderson, Leon. (1993). *Down on Their Luck: A Study of Homeless Street People.* Berkeley, CA: University of California Press.

CHAPTER FOUR

The Social Nature of Individual Lives

Sometimes I run through an area where there are huge houses, an exclusive country club, and a private golf course. The roads in this area are wide, traffic is light, and the spaces between the houses are wooded and green. On the golf course there are ponds where ducks and geese swim and chat. In some ways it is a very pleasant place. But it can also be troubling.

As I run, I wonder why we allow some people to live in mansions while others live in shacks or tenements, or on the street. I get angry at the self-indulgence and waste that I see reflected in houses that are bigger than anyone needs. When I see children in this area, I think of how they will grow up accustomed to comforts and privileges that few people in our society will ever know. And when I see new houses being built, I think of the workers who build these houses but can't afford to buy them.

One time, while running through this area on a hot day, I said hello to two Latino men who were cutting grass in a front yard. They nodded to me but did not return my greeting with any enthusiasm. I thought about my own privileges and how I must look to them. In the middle of the work day, while they cut grass, I was running 5 miles for my own pleasure. They would still be cutting grass when I was home, showered, and in my recliner reading.

A few blocks later two gray-haired men passed me in a golf cart. We were going in the same direction, I on the sidewalk and they to the left of me in the street. Just after they passed me, they turned onto the golf course—right into my path, forcing me to jog around them. They were gabbing away, not seeming to care that they had almost run me over, so I yelled at them: "Wake up and watch where you're going!" They looked surprised and angry. These well-to-do white men were probably not used to being scolded for their misbehavior.

I had gone another mile and was now running in the road, facing traffic, when a car coming toward me slowed and the passenger-side window began to open. I could guess what was about to happen. "Where is the country club?" someone would ask, without even apologizing for interrupting my run. In either direction, the same quick answer sufficed. "Keep going straight. Turn on Lancaster," I would say, without slowing down.

I didn't like being interrupted while running, and having nearly been hit by the men in the golf cart, I did not feel charitable toward lost country clubbers. So when the car slowed, I just waved and kept going. "You aren't really lost," I thought, "just keep driving and you'll find your stupid clubhouse in a minute."

The driver realized that I wasn't going to stop and started to pull away. I glanced inside the car and saw that the driver was a middle-aged black man; the passengers were three plainly dressed black women. It was unlikely that they were country club members. I felt ashamed for not helping them. Thinking that to them I must have seemed like one more white man treating them with disrespect made me feel worse.

When I got home, I thought about how my feelings depended on what had happened during my run. My experience of the run was affected by these brief interactions along the way. I realized that much the same thing occurred whenever I went out. Whether it was to the post office, the grocery store, the coffee shop, the movies, or wherever, interactions always shaped my mood. No doubt my behavior—a hello, a scolding, a snubbing—affected others' moods as well. How might this in turn affect the rest of a person's day? Much could depend on these brief encounters between strangers.

The interactions that occurred during my run were not the products of personalities. Inequality intruded in each case. The Latino men reacted to me as they did in part because of inequalities in our economic positions, and because of inequalities between Anglos and Latinos in this society. The men in the golf cart might have been merely careless, but I suspect it was their social class that led them to expect others to yield the right of way without complaint. My impulse to yell at them, and the pleasure I took in doing so, can probably be traced to my own working-class roots.

Inequality also made a difference when I did not stop for the people who needed directions. If the people in the car had been white, or if I had been black and they white, or if the neighborhood had been different, my passing-by would not have had the same meaning. But because I was white, and because of how whites have mistreated blacks in U.S. society, my behavior could be interpreted as another instance of disrespect. Knowing that my behavior may have hurt the people in the car is what made me feel bad.

Sociological mindfulness can help us see how our feelings depend on what happens in encounters like those on my run. It can also help us see how our emotional responses to these encounters are affected by history, culture, and current social arrangements. We connect with others as we do, in other words, because of the context in which we do it. If we are sociologically mindful, we see that we cannot go through the world disconnected from others, no matter how alone we might feel at times. Even loneliness is a feeling that depends on the state of our relationships with others.

As I've told it, the story of my run is about emotional interdependence, though it also illustrates other kinds of interdependence. I would not have been running at all if I hadn't learned from someone that running is good for my body. I also depended on shoes that let me run without injury. The briefs, shorts, socks, T-shirt, glasses, sweat band, and watch I wore also helped make my run possible—as did the sidewalks and roads on which I ran. And if there had been no clean water coming out of my faucet afterward, I might never have run again. Even though I was running "by myself," I was still connected to others.

We are able to do what we do because of what others have created for us to use. Not only our special activities but our everyday survival depends on getting things through our relationships with others. Even our most creative acts build on, or make use of, ideas and materials that we get from others. Likewise, others depend on us for what they need to live and thrive. Part of being sociologically mindful is paying attention to how these connections are made and to what happens because of them.

Beyond Individualism

People in Western society often fail to see their interdependence. We like to imagine ourselves to be self-reliant individuals, making our way through the world by the strength of talents that are ours alone.

Being sociologically mindful, we can see that this notion is rather silly. If we are going to live as human beings in the modern world, we can no more get by without others than we can get by without air.

Consider the matter of achievement. Typically we think of achievement as resulting from individual effort. We think of people striving to do great things. We then attribute such achievements to the person's special qualities. This way of thinking is seductive because it allows us to create heroes, to take credit for our successes, and to blame others for their failures (rather than noticing our contributions to those failures). But if we are sociologically mindful, we will see that individual achievement is an illusion.

Certainly there are instances of what we call individual achievement. It is just that the achievement is not really individual; it always grows out of a person's ties to others. Suppose that a person from a poor family works hard, overcomes many hardships, and becomes a justice on the U.S. Supreme Court. Isn't this a matter of individual achievement? Not really. It is the result of many relationships and interactions, and it could happen only as a result of many lucky accidents.

To see this, we must not forget the obvious: every judge in black robes was once a baby in diapers. None of us would be alive today if not for the adults who cared for us when we were infants. So there is the first blow to the illusion of individual achievement. We must remember, too, that as children we depended on adults to teach us, encourage us, set examples for us, and help us develop good habits. If they had not done these things, we would not have grown up to be the intelligent, kind, hard-working people we sometimes are.

Achievement also depends on others giving us opportunities to develop and display our abilities. It depends on others being able and willing to recognize the results of our efforts. It depends on powerful others not going out of their way to keep us down. Along the way it depends on others nurturing us, opening doors for us, and giving us time onstage to prove ourselves. If these things don't happen, and happen at the right times, we can't achieve.

Gaining a high social position also requires the existence of institutions. For anyone to become a justice of the Supreme Court, there must be schools, universities, law schools, a federal government, a criminal-justice system, and so on, or there would be no such position to achieve, nor any paths to get there. These institutions exist only because many people continue to do things together in orderly ways. Any individual's achievement thus depends on many other people doing their parts to keep the whole show going.

Achievement also depends on collectively created ideas and values. Why, for instance, would anyone think it worthwhile to strive for power and status in the first place? Why would anyone value such things? How would people know what to do to attain such things? These ideas and values also had to be created, once upon a time, and instilled in individuals. Ambition and cunning are social constructions, too.

People who achieve status and power often do not see what enables their achievement. Perhaps they think, "Yes, I suppose I did get a few breaks along the way, but mostly I have achieved because I am smarter and more determined than others. I am truly a splendid human specimen." This is an illusion fostered by individualism. It is like saying, "See how good I am at climbing this rope? I can do it all by myself"—with no awareness of who taught you to climb, who made the rope, who let it down for you, or who built the place you are climbing to.

Perhaps you would like to believe in genius as a power that springs mysteriously from inside individuals. There are, of course, people whose minds develop rapidly in certain ways. Mozart, for example, wrote symphonies when he was a child and went on to become a great composer. We can marvel at this but still see the need to look beyond Mozart. If Mozart's world had not included pianos, music, and music teachers, he would not have become what he did, at any age.

The same point applies to all instances of genius. A capacity for any kind of performance turns to nothing if the context does not enable its development. No doubt many potential Mozarts have lived and died without ever having seen a piano.

Mindfulness of Interdependence

Students who are striving for success, if only in the form of finding decent jobs when they finish school, are often unmindful of their interdependence. Sometimes they will say, "I am here because of my own merits and will achieve whatever I desire because of my merits. Nothing can stop me." While it is good to be self-confident, it is even better to be self-confident and also to see how we depend on others—past and present—for the nurturing, recognition, and reward of our merits, whatever they might be.

Mindfulness of the social basis of achievement can help us avoid being egotistical, selfish, and ungrateful. It should also help us to feel compassion for those whose chances to live good lives are limited. If we can see how our own achievement depends on ties to others—parents, teachers, friends, life partners, mentors, employers—we should also be able to see that not everyone starts with or can make the same connections and thus may not be able to develop, display, and get rewarded for their abilities. If we can see this, the next step is to look for patterns, that is, to try to see how groups of people are denied chances to do well.

Later I will talk about "seeing patterns." Here I want to say more about being mindful of how social life makes us human. That is what this chapter and the next are about—how our relations of interdependence make us what we are. Even to understand this principle of interdependence depends on our relationships with others.

Consider your reactions to this book. You have probably liked some parts of it and disliked others. Why? It might be hard to say, but it must be because of the ideas and feelings you brought with you to this book. Where did these ideas and feelings come from? The source must be your relationships with others, extending back into your childhood. The implication is that where we stand today—the standpoint from which we react to books or try to understand the world—is a result of our prior and current connections to others.

Philosophers put it this way: "All knowledge is perspectival," which means that we can know about the world only from some point of view. Part of being sociologically mindful is trying to understand how our point of view is a result of our relationships with others. If we are sociologically mindful, we can also see that these relationships are what they are because of the families, schools, social classes, workplaces, ethnic and regional communities, gender groups, nations, and historical times in which we grew up. All this is to say that *what* we know and *how* we know are the results of our ties to others.

Because our knowledge of the world and of ourselves arises from the relationships we have experienced so far in life, we are limited in what we can know about the world and about ourselves, unless we move around a bit. We can literally move around—that is, live in different places, meet new and different people, and learn how they see the world—or we can use our minds to move around. We can read about other people's experiences and ideas. Looking back on ourselves from these other points of view, we might see things we never imagined.

Perspectives and Groups

Sociological mindfulness means recognizing not only that there are other points of view, but that these points of view are linked to groups and to the position of groups relative to each other. Consider teachers, for instance. They come to share ideas, a way of talking, and a general outlook because they do similar kinds of work and face similar problems in doing it. Teachers also learn from each other about how to deal with students, parents, secretaries, principals, school boards, and so on.

Teachers face similar problems because of how schools are organized and how teachers are positioned relative to the other groups that are part of the scene. If schools were reorganized so that teachers were in charge, that would change the way groups relate to each other and would no doubt lead teachers and others in the system to develop different perspectives. A perspective thus takes shape because of commonalities (in this case, among teachers) and differences (between teachers and others in the education system).

To take another example, as long as doctors relate to patients, nurses, administrators, and each other in ways that are determined by how hospitals are organized, doctors will tend to face similar problems and develop a shared perspective. It is not that all doctors, any more than all teachers, think alike in every detail. The point is that people who do similar kinds of work, solve similar kinds of problems, earn their money in similar ways, and relate to others in similar ways will tend to develop a shared outlook on the world.

When I want students to think about the dangers of masculinity, I will say, "Every man in the room can probably imagine circumstances in which he would feel compelled to kill another man, so as to prove his own manhood." The men look grim and nod their heads. Then I ask the women, "Can you imagine having to kill another woman to prove that you are a woman?" They just stare back because the question makes no sense in light of how we define "womanhood" in our culture. Where is the interdependence here? It is between women and men. We can see this if we recognize that men are constructed to be what women are not.

In our culture, men are supposed to be capable of violence; women are not (even though, in fact, some women can be quite violent). To be a respected member of the category "men," it is necessary, under some conditions, to threaten or to commit violence. Men know, even if they do not say it, that violence may be necessary to avoid being treated like a woman—which would mean being dominated by other men. When I ask for examples of times when a man might have to fight to prove he is a man, someone usually says, "If, like, another guy called you a woman."

What is important to see here is the interdependence between the gender categories that give rise to different perspectives. "Men" and "women" are complementary categories, usually fashioned as opposites. In this sense the categories are interdependent—neither would make sense without the other. If we did not create the categories "women" and "men" and enforce the idea that, to be a man, one must not show the weakness, softness, and passivity defined as women's traits, then men would not know what they know about manly honor and killing.

If we did not create groups of people called "women" and "men," and if we did not segregate them and teach them different ways to be human, they would not be much different at all. But our society is organized so that women and men typically experience different kinds of tasks, hardships, and pleasures. Men thus know and feel things that women do not, and women know and feel things that men do not. These differences in knowledge and feelings are not natural, but rather the results of how the categories "women" and "men" are defined and of how the people in these categories are taught to think, feel, and act.

Again, it is not that all men think alike, feel alike, or agree with each other, nor that all men are totally different from women. These things are obviously not true. Yet it is true that knowing one's self as a man, and knowing the world from the standpoint of a man, is possible only because of the interdependent categories "women" and "men" to which males and females are assigned. What sociological mindfulness helps us to see in this case is that our "individual" point of view—as a man or a woman—is really a result of how we learn to relate to others.

Understanding Ourselves by Understanding Others

The nature of our ties to others can keep us from understanding important things about ourselves and others. Consider the example of blacks and whites in the United States. Which group is likely to know more about the other? It seems likely that blacks will know more about whites than whites know about blacks. Why? Because whites have been more powerful (politically and economically) than blacks, so blacks have had to watch whites carefully, just to survive.

It is like this: If you are a worker, you must pay attention to what your boss is thinking and feeling, because your job depends on being able to anticipate his or her behavior. Good bosses will pay attention to what workers think and feel, but that is not the point. Because of a boss's power, a worker has more incentive to study the boss than the boss has to study the worker. After all, if a worker doesn't do a good job of anticipating what the boss wants, the boss can fire a worker. A worker can't fire the boss.

In the history of the United States, blacks have not been able to "fire" whites who enslaved, abused, or disrespected them. Blacks have not had the power to do that. And so, to survive and avoid trouble, blacks have had to study whites more closely than whites have had to study blacks. The average black person is thus likely to know more about whites and about "white culture" than the average white person knows about blacks and about "black culture." This is an example of how inequalities between groups can shape, or limit, the knowledge that people in those groups come to possess.

To push the example, consider this question: Do blacks know more about whites than whites know about themselves? The answer is most likely yes, because learning about ourselves requires taking the perspectives of others. We must, in other words, be able to see ourselves as others see us. If we have a great deal of power—relative to other persons or groups—then we are unlikely to concern ourselves with how others see us.

Most white people do not try very hard to see themselves through the eyes of black people. This is not to say that whites willfully ignore the perspectives of blacks. More likely, it never occurs to most whites to look at themselves from the perspectives of blacks, since whites have no compelling reasons to do so. Likewise, most Americans rarely look at themselves through the eyes of people in other countries. The economic and military power of the United States allows Americans to ignore what people in other countries think.

The principle here concerns power and knowledge. If groups are unequal to each other, this affects what members of those groups are likely to know about each other and how hard they will try to know each other. Those in more powerful groups will generally know less about people in less powerful groups. Powerful people are even likely to know less about themselves, in some ways, than the powerless know about them. It is as if the cost of power is ignorance about one's self and others.

Relations of inequality are also relations of interdependence. One group may be stronger than another, yet still depend on the other. Masters need slaves just as capitalists need workers. As people in dominant and subordinate groups struggle to survive—recognizing that the struggle may be much harder for one group than for the other—they create the conditions and experiences that lead some people to know what others do not. The knowledge that individuals acquire depends largely on which group they are in and how their group cooperates and competes with other groups.

A second principle is thus that "individual" knowledge is always a social product. What we know depends on the nature of our relationships with others. Part of being sociologically mindful is getting beyond individualism and appreciating how those relationships make us what we are. By doing so we can discover the limits of our knowledge and see how to increase it in ways that will allow us to live more responsibly in the world.

"Personal" Choices

If you had younger brothers or sisters, your parents probably urged you to set a good example for them. In telling you this, your parents were trying to make you mindful of a kind of interdependence. They wanted you to be aware that your behavior could affect others who learned from watching you. Otherwise you might have thought that your behavior was purely a matter of "personal choice," with no sense that your choices could help or harm others.

Sociological mindfulness, in contrast, means paying attention to how our behaviors affect, and are affected by, others. We might thereby see that many of our choices are not so personal, in that they have significant bearing on others, directly or indirectly. It is not always easy to see how this is so, and in some cases we may not want to see.

I said earlier that being mindful of the consequences of our actions does not mean trying to imagine all possible consequences. That would keep us from acting at all. The best we can do is to imagine the consequences that are *likely*, in light of how the social world works. Sociological mindfulness does not prescribe or prohibit any particular choices. Being mindful is a matter of taking more things into account before we act. If we do that, we may very well decide to act differently, depending on what we value.

In chapter 1 I used the example of working in destructive jobs. Sociological mindfulness, I said, can help us see the harm that arises from working in such jobs, perhaps leading us to try to earn a living differently. Below are several more examples of that kind, although not about jobs. In each case I am suggesting what we might see if we are mindful of our interdependence with others.

Smoking

If you are a smoker, you might defend your habit on the grounds that it is a personal choice. Perhaps you think that even if smoking harms your body, it is *your* body to do with as you please. Perhaps you think that as long as you bear the costs of your addiction and do not blow smoke in anyone's face, then it is no one's business but your own. That is the kind of thinking encouraged by individualism, which inhibits a mindful assessment of how your habit affects others.

As a smoker you are setting a bad example for children and others who might look up to you. Your behavior says that smoking is okay and not really harmful, or else why would you do it? If you smoke outside and drop your cigarette butts on the ground, as most smokers do, you are also communicating a disrespect for public space and for the earth. And if you smoke in any enclosed space, such as an airport or a restaurant, even if smoking is allowed, you are harming other people's health, even if they do not complain.

There is more to consider. For example, when you buy cigarettes you are helping to get others addicted—not only because of the example you set, but because you provide tobacco companies with funds for advertising. This is like donating money to drug dealers to help them persuade children, especially teenagers, that drug use is sexy, glamorous, and a sign of adult sophistication. Your choice to smoke thus has, as one consequence, the harm done to others who are duped into becoming users themselves.

Even if you smoked stolen cigarettes in a closet, you could not avoid harming others. Consider that health insurance costs more for everyone because smokers require extra care to treat their various smoking-related diseases. Your choice to smoke imposes these costs on others. And if you are disabled by emphysema or die early because of lung cancer or a heart attack, your family and friends may be deeply anguished. In this way you force them to pay for your choice, which, if you can see it mindfully, is not personal at all.

If you think that I think smoking is a bad idea, you are right, though what I have said here is not an argument against smoking. It is an illustration of what sociological mindfulness calls us to consider when we presume to make personal choices. If we are sociologically mindful, we see that it is possible, sometimes, for our choices to have effects that travel far beyond us. Part of being mindful is trying to discern the effects that arise because of our interdependence with others.

Violent Sports

Here is another example of a harmful choice, one that might strike you as strange: watching football. Perhaps you are thinking, "Football? He has gone too far! What could be wrong with football? It doesn't cause lung cancer or heart disease. It's just fun!" It is true that, other than injuries to players, football doesn't cause physical disease. But it does contribute to several diseases of social life: authoritarianism, militarism, and sexism.

If we say that football is "just another game in which athletes compete with each other for prizes," we are ignoring the crucial particulars. Football is not just any game, but one that calls for violence and thus places a premium on size, strength, and force. Yes, it also calls for strategy and skill, and in this sense it is like many other games. But then we should ask, "To what ends are strategy, skill, and force put in the game of football?" The answer is in the game itself: The goal is to penetrate the farthest limits of the opposing team's territory (achieving a touchdown or field goal). It takes no great interpretive skill to see this as a metaphorical enactment of war.

So, then, what does sociological mindfulness lead us to see when we watch a football game? We could say, "Ah, we see a metaphorical enactment of war." But we could say, more simply, that what we see are groups of beefy men striving to dominate each other. Then we can widen our view and note that we also see women on the sidelines, cheering for the men as they perform the serious action; we see fans shrieking and yelling in delight when "their team" crushes the other; and we see that the action is directed by a few male commanders—coaches and quarterbacks.

Seen in this way, football is not only a metaphorical enactment of war; it is a microcosm of social life on our planet. Men struggle with each other for power, a few elite men ordering other men to do the violent dirty work; women keep out of the way, providing support and decoration; and most people, lacking any power themselves, just watch and cheer.

You might accept all this and still enjoy football. Really, what could be the harm? The answer is that participating in the spectacle of football, if only as a casual viewer, reinforces the same values and impulses that underlie war and men's domination of women. It does so by implying that a violent struggle for masculine power is fine entertainment. People may not intend to imply any such thing; they may intend only to be amused by the game. Their behavior nonetheless signifies the acceptability of the values encoded in the game.

Imagine, in contrast, what a conscientious objector to football might say: "I will have nothing to do with this game—not even lend it legitimacy by watching it—because football makes violence and domination, and the devaluation of women, seem normal and acceptable." The objector is mindful of how deeds can reinforce ideas and values, because deeds, such as watching football, convey messages. And so the objector chooses not to convey to others the message that the values encoded in football are okay.

Having Babies

Here is another example that pushes even farther into the territory of what we usually consider personal choice: women having babies. I do not propose to consider all the circumstances under which women might choose to have babies. I have in mind the case where an educated young woman, perhaps a college graduate, gets married, works for several years, and then quits working to have babies and live primarily off her husband's income. This is a common pattern among heterosexual women in the United States.

If such a young woman wants to get married, work for a while, and then quit to stay at home and raise children, isn't that a choice she should be free to make? Yes, of course—just as people should be free to smoke and to watch football if that is what they want to do, after considering the consequences as fully as possible. Sociological mindfulness demands only mindfulness, not any particular course of action.

So what should a young woman be mindful of if she is considering having babies? Consider how her situation might unfold. Because women tend to be channeled into lower-paying, lower-status jobs than men, it is likely, first of all, that her job will be less rewarding than her husband's. Her paid work may not feel especially meaningful, either. Under these conditions, the option of raising children may be attractive. It is a way to avoid the hassles of the workplace, a way to do something meaningful, and a way to achieve adult status as a woman. It may also be a way to end nagging by parents: "So, when are you going to have children?"

If she quits her job to have babies, several consequences are likely to follow. One is that her boss, who is likely to be a man, will think, "Yes, this is what I feared would happen. We invest time and energy in training these women and after a few years they quit to have babies. I guess that is just their nature. In the future I will try to put men in these jobs and promote them faster, since men are likely to be more committed to their work." This kind of thinking on the part of an employer could have bad consequences for other women in the workplace.

A woman who quits her job is also likely to lose power in the home. This happens in part because she becomes economically dependent on her husband. Now her husband can say, "I go out into the world every day to earn the money that keeps this household afloat. I take my lumps out there. So I think my preferences deserve extra consideration when it comes to making decisions around here." Even if he doesn't say exactly this, it would be surprising if he didn't believe it. And whether we think this belief is right or wrong, it is not crazy, economically, to give extra weight to the needs of the person whose income supports the family.

So now she stays home to cook and clean and raise the children. He may help out occasionally, but because he is the breadwinner for the family, he must work all the harder at his job. He may thus have little time for what he sees as the trivia of housework. "Besides," he might think, "isn't that supposed to be *her* contribution to the family? If I earn the money to support us, she ought to keep up the house and tend to the kids. I have more important things to worry about." Perhaps the woman accepts this arrangement because it helps her husband get ahead at work, which means more money for the family. It is an arrangement that has other costs, but she sees it as her personal choice.

To begin to see the unintended consequences of this choice, consider her husband's workplace competitors. Who are the ones least likely to have wives providing support at home? Women. Lacking wives, women are less able to dedicate themselves fully to work. Bosses thus get the impression that men are better employees, especially at higher ranks, because they will be more dedicated—more willing to "stay late and get the job done." One consequence, then, of a woman's choice to stay home, raise kids, and nurture a husband is the perpetuation of gender inequality at work. To say it another way, one consequence is to limit women's chances of getting ahead.

You might think, "If a woman does not want to impede her career by having children, she should just not have children, and perhaps stay single as well. Then she will be able to match the men at work." Of course. Suppose, however, that most of the men with whom a single or childfree woman works have economically dependent, stay-at-home wives. If these men are used to dealing with their wives as "junior partners," will they be able to accept women as equals and superiors at work? Or are these men likely to think that a woman's place is in the home, where her job is to service a man's needs? Under such conditions, men may come to presume that the workplace is a man's domain. They may also come to presume that the service and deference they get from their wives at home is what they are entitled to receive from women in general.

A husband and wife are obviously interdependent, emotionally and financially. That is easy to see. What is not so easy to see is how *women* are interdependent, such that the "personal choices" of women who stay home to have babies have consequences for women who are striving for equality in the workplace. If we are mindful of how our society works, we can see that when women give up their economic independence and stake themselves on a relationship to a man, they are perpetuating disadvantages for other women. And not only this, for when a woman wishes to return to work, out of need or desire, she will find those disadvantages waiting for her.

I have heard women students say, "I really dislike it that feminism says that if you stay home and raise children, you are bad." When I ask why they think any feminist would say such a thing, these students say, "It's because they see housework as demeaning." This is quite wrong. It is actually men who see housework as trivial and demeaning, which is why they don't want to do it. Nor do feminists say that women who take care of homes and children are bad (actually, feminists have argued that caring and nurturing are valuable and important).

What feminists have done is to urge women to be mindful of how their choices affect other women. To opt for having babies simply because that is what women are expected to do, or because of a stalled career, is not to make a mindful choice. It is to be pulled back to a deeply rutted path that most likely leads away from equality for women in our society. Again, to be sociologically mindful about these matters does not preclude choosing to have children. It means recognizing the interdependencies that make this a choice with far-reaching social, rather than merely personal, consequences.

A Scientist's Dilemma

Suppose that you are a scientist who needs money to do a research project. Suppose that a foundation is willing to fund your project. Suppose that this foundation is associated with a tobacco company, such that its money comes from the sales of cigarettes. Would you take the money? Before deciding, you would probably want to consider why the foundation gives money to support research and what it hopes to gain by doing so.

Why does a company "give away" some of its money? The answer is to make the company and its products appear legitimate. It is really a form of advertising. If you take the money, you are helping the company appear respectable. Taking the money would mean that it is no big deal if it comes from selling a drug that injures and kills people. You would be saying, in effect, that this is not worth worrying about. You would thus be helping the company stay in business by aiding its claim to be a useful "corporate citizen."

If you were the scientist in this case, you might find it hard to be sociologically mindful. You might be inclined to exaggerate the possible benefits of your project and rationalize taking the money: "If I don't take it, someone else will. At least I'll do some good with it." That may be true; some good might come of your project.

But is it realistic to expect this possible good to offset the harm done to millions of people whose health will be damaged and who will die prematurely because they are tricked into smoking? Making tobacco companies seem legitimate and respectable is part of the trick. Being honestly mindful of this, you might work harder to find money for your project from another source.

Re-examining Our Choices

When we call smoking, watching football, having babies, or taking money from any legal source a "personal choice," we mask our interdependence with others. It is as if to deny that these behaviors have any effect on others, and to say that no one has a right to challenge us about these behaviors. Sociological mindfulness is in part the practice of re-examining our choices, paying special attention to how our choices have consequences for others.

When faced with choices, people sometimes look at the option toward which they are inclined and say, "Why not? I don't see any reason why I *shouldn't* do X, so I guess I will, since X is most appealing to me." But what this often means is, "I don't want to, or don't know how to, think any more about the consequences of doing X, so I'll go ahead with X." This is not a mindful way to proceed.

We always come to a point, in any case, where we have considered all that we know how to consider. If we are sociologically mindful, it will take longer to get to that point because we will be considering more connections and interdependencies. We will also be trying to look at our choices from a range of perspectives. This will take extra time, too, since we need to talk to others, or read what they have written, to learn how to examine our choices from new perspectives.

Being mindful may slow us down, but it does not diminish our choices. It may in fact lead us to see choices that we previously missed. It also equips us to make well-considered choices that reflect our best values. Being mindful of connections and interdependence can thus help us make real individual choices, not the kind that merely seem to be individual because they are conveniently defined as "personal."

Then again, individuals are not solely responsible for the results of their acts. Interdependence means that our acts have the consequences they do because of how the social world works. Women ought to be able to have babies without reproducing gender inequality. Scientists ought to be able to fund their projects without prostituting themselves. If these things are not possible, it is not because individuals are immoral, but because of the conditions under which they act. Being sociologically mindful is a way to see more clearly what these conditions are and to see how we can act responsibly in spite of them.

RELATED READINGS

Bellah, Robert N., Madsen, Richard, Sullivan, William M., Swidler, Ann, & Tipton, Steven M. (1985). *Habits of the Heart: Individualism and Commitment in American Life*. Berkeley, CA: University of California Press.

Dewey, John. (1908/1932). *Theory of the Moral Life*. New York: Holt, Rinehart and Winston.

Gilligan, Carol. (1982). *In a Different Voice*. Cambridge, MA: Harvard University Press.

Nhat Hanh, Thich. (1987). *Interbeing*. Berkeley, CA: Parallax Press.

Noddings, Nel. (1984). *Caring*. Berkeley, CA: University of California Press.

Rubin, Lillian. (1983). *Intimate Strangers*. New York: Harper & Row.

■ ■ ■ ■ ■ ■ ■ ■ ■ ■ ■ ■ ■ ■

Becoming Human

To do the experiment I am going to describe, we would need a pair of newborn identical twins. We would also need a large box in which one of the twins could live without contact with other humans. The box would have to deliver food and water, and remove waste, mechanically. It would also have to be opaque and soundproof, so that there could be no interaction through its walls.

The experiment is simple: One child is raised normally and the other is put in the box. After 18 years we open the box and compare the two children to see if they are any different. If they are, we can conclude that being with other people matters. If both children are the same after 18 years, we have to conclude that socialization (learning from being with other people) makes little difference and that personality is genetically programmed.

You might think, "Of course socialization makes a difference. We don't need to raise a child in a box to prove that!" But there are many people who argue that what a person becomes depends on his or her genes. If that's true, then it shouldn't matter if a child is raised in a box. Genetic programming should turn the child into whatever s/he was destined to become, inside or outside the box.

It would be wrong, of course, to do the box experiment, since one baby would be denied experiences that we value in our culture: intimacy, physical affection, and mental stimulation. We value these things precisely because we know how crucial they are to creating decent human beings. Merely imagining the box experiment shocks us into remembering this.

But not everyone is mindful of how social life makes us human. One time, after a discussion about how children are taught to be girls and boys, a male student said, "My mom taught me to sew and cook, and my dad taught me to hunt and fish. My sisters learned to do all these things, too." His point wasn't clear, so I asked, "Are you saying that you were biologically wired to become the man you are, regardless of what your parents taught you?" He said yes, that's what he was getting at.

At the next class meeting I told this student about his twin brother, Fester, who had been sold to unscrupulous experimenters right after birth. "He lived the first 18 years of his life in a box," I said, "and when the box was opened, it was a sad sight. Fester cowered like a helpless, terrified animal, unable to speak or reason. You did not know about the comparisons that were made between you and him because they were done secretly, by video. The judgments were made by a team of scientists who reviewed the tapes and determined that—" At which point another student chimed in, "—there were no differences!" Even poor Fester's brother laughed.

The joke made the point that it is rather silly to think that anyone could "just turn out" to be a well-functioning adult. If that were so, parents could save themselves a great deal of trouble by raising their children in boxes.

In real life the nature-versus-nurture debate is unresolvable. Every person develops as s/he does because some potentials are nurtured while others are not. Without social life, no potentials would be developed; a different social life would develop different potentials; and if the potentials aren't there, nothing can develop them. So there is really no separating the contributions of nature and nurture to making us what we are. Everyone is a result of the interaction between these two influences.

To be sociologically mindful of how we become human, we need presume only this: Everyone has more potential than will be realized. This means that what we become as individuals—the abilities, desires, and habits that make us who we are—is just the realization of one set of possibilities. We can't really know what all our potentials are; we can only know, late in life, which ones have been realized. What we can know, or at least be mindful of, is how social life turns us into certain kinds of people.

To see this, we must be mindful of our interdependencies. But there is more to it. We must also pay attention to how society is organized, where we fit into it, and how our place in it gives rise to experiences that make us what we are. This "socialness" includes all that makes us more than animals: the workings of our minds, the possession of self-consciousness, our desires and hopes, and our feelings about ourselves. All of these things about us, these qualities that make us human, arise out of social life.

Not everyone wants to know how this happens. Some people, like Fester's brother, resist being sociologically mindful of how we become human. Why? Perhaps because we are taught, in American culture, that our worth depends on being unique individuals—while being mindful of how we are shaped by social life makes us seem less special. Since a lot of other people have been shaped in similar ways, to reflect on this fact may make us feel like undistinguished members of the common horde.

Are we just like others? In some ways, yes. We have had similar experiences, hold similar attitudes, values, and beliefs, and do similar things. This is what we would expect when people grow up in the same culture. In some ways we are slightly different from others— not a lot different, just a little. And in still other ways we may be unique. No one else has had exactly the same experiences we have had, no one else has been shaped in exactly the way we have, and no one else lives inside our skins.

It is the case, then, that we are both one of a kind and of a kind. We are both different from and the same as others. Often in U.S. culture we exaggerate our differences and fail to be mindful of what we have in common with others.

An old Chinese proverb says, "The first step to becoming an individual is to recognize that you are not one." This means that as long as we cling to an illusion of individuality—without examining how we are like and unlike others—we will fail to become all that we could become as individuals. It is as if the illusion of being unique is so satisfying that it stops us from doing the kind of thinking that helps us grow as people. The proverb also reminds us that our similarities with others are essential to being human.

The point of being mindful of these matters is not to help us strive toward individuality, as if that were the highest goal of a human life. The point is to be mindful of how we make ourselves and others human, as a step toward doing it with more wisdom and compassion. Being sociologically mindful is a way to see how what we become as people depends on the nature of our ties to others. We can thus see, perhaps, how we can do things together in ways that make human beings more able and willing to create good lives for themselves and for others.

Gathering Meanings

You are lucky not to have grown up in a box. Instead you have learned from other human beings a language that allows you to get a mental grip on the world. For you the world is not a confusing blur but a place that makes sense, a place full of meaningful events, situations, and objects (including yourself and other people). Without language all this would be lost. You would be trapped in a world without meaning.

What makes us able to live together as humans? It is our ability to solve problems peacefully and creatively; our ability to build elaborate institutions and traditions; our ability to share experiences with each other; our ability to preserve knowledge over time; and our ability to imagine and talk about the future. We couldn't do these things without language, which gives us the power to develop our individual humanity and to connect with others in distinctly human ways. If you are mindful of the power of language, you will want to pay close attention to its nature and use. To do so is to be mindful of how human beings create themselves and a shared social world.

Taking on Identities

As an infant you did not know that the sound you heard over and again was your name, though eventually you learned that "Mal" or "Rosa" was a sound that referred to you and you alone. In learning your name, you became aware of yourself as an object. You learned that you were a creature that could be talked about, thought about, praised, scolded, loved, hated, and so on. As soon as you were able to think, "I am so-and-so," you began to gather meanings to yourself and become a complex being.

As we grow up, we gather meanings to ourselves from the culture in which we live. This means learning to define ourselves using the terms available in our culture. Others must teach us which terms to use and when. These meanings we gather—identities such as student, biology major, son or daughter, Democrat, liberal, Christian or Buddhist, black or white, gay or straight, baby boomer or generation Xer—give us a sense of who we are. This is part of becoming human, this process of coming to know who and what we are.

Being sociologically mindful, we see that the meanings we give to ourselves always arise out of social life. We depend on each other not only to define ourselves, but also to maintain a coherent and stable sense of who and what we are as persons. If others didn't help us sustain our identity claims, we would have a hard time knowing for sure who and what we really are.

Our identities—the meanings we give to ourselves and announce to others—locate us relative to others and tell them how to treat us. Announcing our identities allows others to interact with us in predictable ways. If others know you are a plumber, for instance, they will know how to treat you in certain situations—like when a pipe is leaking. Identities are thus not private meanings that rattle around inside our heads. Identities are public meanings that determine much of what goes on between people.

You might gather other meanings that work the same way. If others know that you are "short-tempered," or "rich," or "good-humored," they will know something about how to interact with you. In gathering meanings to ourselves we thus acquire many possible points of connection—that is, many ways that others can see who and what we are and thus interact with us predictably and smoothly. Social life not only gives us our identities; it depends on them.

Identities let us interpret ourselves to others quickly. When you say, "I am a student," or "I am a biology major," or "I am an engineer," you are using a shorthand way of telling others who and what you are. Not everyone grasps the meaning of "student" or "biology major" or "engineer" in the same way. Even so, such an identity is a handy starting point. After claiming an identity, we usually go on to interpret ourselves to others. We try, in lots of ways, to influence the meanings others give to us.

Acquiring language and developing self-awareness are essential to becoming human and to being able to function in the social world. Gathering meanings to one's self—that is, becoming known to one's self and to others as a particular kind of person—is also part of becoming human. Being sociologically mindful, we can see that these processes happen only because of interaction. We cannot become human in a box. Who and what we become depends on the symbols and meanings, and opportunities to use them, that social life affords. We are no less interdependent in becoming human than in being human.

Regulating Ourselves

Fester's brother might have taken offense at the joke about "no differences" and gone berserk. Fortunately, he laughed with the rest of us. How come? Why didn't he go berserk? He must have developed some ability that allowed him to regulate his behavior so as to be a safe and useful participant in social life. If people do not become self-regulating in this way, they can cause a lot of trouble.

Language and self-awareness are prerequisites to being self-regulating. But they are not enough. We must develop several other distinctly human characteristics.

First, we must become attached to the meanings we gather to ourselves. We become attached to them because they provide a sense of coherence and continuity. You are today your mother's son or daughter, just as you were yesterday. This knowledge, along with knowledge of your other identities, keeps you sane by allowing you to be comfortably sure of who and what you are from one day to the next.

It is even better if you are attached to some identities because you (and others) value those identities highly. If this is true, these valued identities will be a source of self-esteem. This is another reason you might be attached to them. Perhaps, too, the more self-esteem you have staked on a particular identity, the more firmly you will be attached to it.

What does this have to do with self-regulation? If you are attached to your identities, you will try to act in ways that uphold them. If you think of yourself as, for example, an honest person, and then have a chance to cheat on a test, you might decide not to cheat, so as to be able to continue to see yourself as an honest person. If you think of yourself as a good student, and this self-conception is important to you, you will tend to do things that good students do: read, think, ask questions, attend class, complete assignments on time, and so on. These behaviors say to you and to others that you are indeed a good student.

If we are attached to certain ideas about ourselves, we will tend to do things that affirm rather than contradict those ideas. We will try to behave in ways that lead others to see us as we would like to see ourselves. For instance, if "friendly person" is an important identity for someone, s/he will probably repress impulses to grouch at people or to remain aloof, so as to avoid discrepant feedback from others: "You grouch, you are not very friendly!" The identity, whatever it might be, and as long as we care about embracing it, becomes a device for regulating our own behavior.

Being self-regulating also depends on learning criteria for self-evaluation. Generally, we want to feel good about ourselves, so we will try to do things that attest to our competence and morality. What these things are depends on the culture, the situation, and the identity a person is claiming. For example, a man might learn that, when dealing with children, a good man is patient, kind, and generous. If he can exhibit these qualities, he will be able to evaluate himself highly and thus maintain self-esteem.

Not all criteria for self-evaluation are so benign. In U.S. culture, a man might also learn that a real man is powerful, aggressive, competitive, and in control. He may thus feel compelled to try to exhibit these qualities so as to feel good about himself as a man. If he goes too far, his behavior is likely to cause harm to others.

Fortunately, Fester's brother seemed to think of himself as the kind of man who was strong enough to take a little teasing and enjoy a joke at his own expense. If he had seen himself as the kind of man whose strength lay in using violence to punish anyone who affronted his dignity, the situation might have turned out badly.

You can see why it is necessary to be careful about the criteria for self-evaluation that we teach children—and why we should critically examine the criteria we apply to ourselves. The danger otherwise is that we will come to stake our feelings of competence and worth on being good at things that produce bad results for others.

We should be glad that for most people being a good person means being honest, kind, generous, compassionate, and peaceful. Having learned these criteria for self-evaluation, people are nicer and easier to get along with. To put it another way, most people avoid doing things that are dishonest, cruel, selfish, callous, and violent so as to avoid seeing themselves as rotten. This makes people self-regulating in a useful way. If people learn to seek self-esteem by treating others well, then they are more likely to behave like decent human beings.

Silent Knowledge

Self-regulation also requires being equipped with knowledge of how to interact with others in various situations. This knowledge is usually unspoken; it is a matter of knowing how to do something without necessarily being able to explain it. We rely on a great deal of this kind of silent knowledge to get through everyday life.

For example, you probably know how to go into a store, find the best deal on tofu and eggplant, make your purchase, and leave. You probably also know how to line up to buy tickets, how to behave at a funeral, how to make small talk at parties, how to dress yourself in the morning, how to behave on a first date, how to deal with your boss, how to ask for and give directions, how to blow your nose in public, and so on. These might seem like simple acts, but that is only because we forget how much knowledge they require.

Imagine programming a robot to mail a letter. At first it might seem that only two instructions are needed: "Put stamp on envelope. Put envelope in mailbox." But robots are stupid, so you'd have to provide more explicit instructions. You'd have to say what a stamp is, how to choose the right kind of stamp, what an envelope is, where to put a stamp on an envelope, what a mailbox is, where to find one, how to put an envelope in it, and so on. Your robot would need to know all this.

Eventually your list of instructions might run to hundreds, perhaps thousands, of lines. Even more amazing than the effort it would take to program a robot to do a job as "simple" as mailing a letter is the fact that you have all this knowledge in your head, already. Imagine someone trying to program a robot to do all the things you know how to do. It is unlikely that all that knowledge—billions of lines of instructions?—could be put into a form any less complex than the brain itself.

Just as one more example of silent knowledge, think of what you must know to be able to speak a sentence in the English language. Can you explain how to do it, how to get all the right words in the right order so that a coherent sentence comes out of your mouth? Probably not. But still you know how. Somehow.

Knowing how to interact with others is much the same. Just as we need to know the rules of English to formulate proper sentences, we need to know the rules of social life to be able to fit our actions together into coherent wholes.

Some of the rules we need to know are normative, such as "Do not treat other human beings as objects," or "Always respect other people's feelings." These rules tell us what is right and wrong and how to behave morally. Other rules are procedural; they tell us how to make situations unfold in the ways we want them to.

If everyone knows the same procedural rules, we can smoothly go about our business of buying eggplant and tofu, lining up for tickets, driving in traffic, having conversations, falling in love, running universities, and so on. Each of us will have a rough idea of how to proceed when we try to do things together. Once we are equipped with the procedural rules needed to handle routine situations, we can carry on our lives without having to call home for instructions. In other words, we become self-regulating.

These rules do not control us from the inside. Rather, they are resources we use to get things done with other people. Sometimes we get things done by breaking a rule.

Suppose, for example, a rule says, "Do not stare at people." When walking down a busy street you use this rule to avoid attracting the attention of strangers. You hope that if you avoid eye contact, strangers will not feel invited to annoy you. Under other conditions—perhaps someone invades your space on the bus—you might break the rule against staring so as to say, "Please get away from me." In this case you stare as a way to send a message. This works because people know the rule against staring and know that breaking it is meaningful.

Keeping Things on Track

Basic rules of interaction will get us through most situations. But problems can arise when it's not clear, or not clear to everyone, exactly what the situation is, or when people disagree about the rules that ought to be used in a given situation. For these and other reasons interaction can go awry. Somehow we must be able to get things back on track.

We do this, most obviously, through talk. In cases of confusion or conflict—when someone doesn't seem to know what's going on, or doesn't behave properly, or rejects our understanding of what's going on—we can usually talk our way to some kind of solution. We have to do more, however, than talk. We must also be able to take the perspectives of others. This means imagining what they are thinking, feeling, and likely to do.

It is crucial that we learn to read others in this way. We have to be able to look at others' circumstances and think, "How would *I* feel if I were in that kind of situation? How would *I* be likely to act?" Sometimes we must make inferences from others' speech and appearance. We might think, "She is slouching, unkempt, not looking me in the eye, and sounding very tired and sad—she is probably depressed." I am exaggerating a bit here; the signs of a person's inner state are often more subtle. In any case, we must learn how to "see inside" others, so we can anticipate how they will behave and what they expect from us.

Doing things together requires us to be able to read people in these ways. Navigating our way through the social world requires not only that we be equipped with rules for interacting in standard situations. We must also be able to deal with unusual situations where it is necessary to figure out how strangers are thinking and feeling. Talk and perspective-taking are the best means we have of figuring out how to proceed.

Feeling for and with Others

Perhaps I have made it seem that self-regulation depends solely on reason, so that if people just think straight they will be gentle and considerate. There is, however, more to it than that. Reason is not enough to keep us from hurting ourselves and others. As history has shown, human beings can always think of ways to make cruelty and violence seem reasonable. So logic and rational argument are not enough to ensure that humans will behave humanely. What is also necessary is the ability, and willingness, to feel for and with others.

I am referring to what might be called "perspective-taking with the heart"—allowing ourselves to respond emotionally to others. Our responses can be sympathetic (feeling *for* an other) or empathic (feeling *with* an other). If we feel sorry for a friend whose parent has died, that is a sympathetic response. If we feel some of the friend's grief, as if our own parent had died, that is an empathic response. In either case we experience feelings in response to the other person's feelings. Such responses are not automatic; we can refuse to have them.

Imagine you have a chance to steal a pot of money that has been donated to buy medicine for poor children. The money is right there, unguarded. You could use it to pay bills, buy a new stereo, and have a spot of fun. The chances of getting caught are slim. How will you decide whether or not to take the money?

You might try to imagine how stealing the money would make others feel. The people who donated and collected it would be angry. The children who expected to benefit from it would be sad, discouraged, and made to suffer for lack of the medicine they need. If you were caught and sent to trial, then your family and friends would feel shame and disappointment. You would probably also feel disgust for yourself. If you can imagine all this and let yourself feel what others would feel if you stole the money, you will probably leave it alone.

But suppose that your mind is quicker than your heart, and before you feel anything you think, "The people who gave this money are rich and just looking for a tax deduction; they don't really care about poor children. As for the kids, I'm sure they'll find help somewhere. Besides, most medicines don't do any good at all; you're better off not taking them. I doubt that much of the money even goes to the kids at all. It probably goes into administrators' pockets. Those folks already have more money than they need. I don't. I'm broke. This money will do me a lot more good than it will do them. I'll just scoop it up and be on my way."

In the second case you would have convinced yourself, quite rationally, that taking the money is a reasonable thing to do. There is even some perspective-taking involved: "The rich don't really care about poor children." That might be true, though it cannot justify taking the money, since other people's feelings are also at stake. It is only by ignoring these feelings that reason is allowed to proceed to a hurtful conclusion.

It is not just to deter hurtful acts that we must feel with and for others. Ordinary interaction also depends on emotional responsiveness. Consider, for example, the ritual greeting we usually enact when we pass someone we know: "Hi, how're you?" "Fine, how're you?" "Good." "That's good." "See you later." "See you." It seems that there is little thought or feeling in this exchange. So why do we do it? What purpose does it serve?

The greeting ritual is a way for people to acknowledge each other's presence. We do this because we know it feels better to have one's existence affirmed than to be ignored. We do it, in other words, because we respect other people's feelings, and they ours. It is a little ritual that uplifts and stabilizes us emotionally as we go through our days. Imagine how you would feel if everyone to whom you said, "Hi, how're you?" either did not reply or said, "Bug off."

Small acts of politeness serve the same purpose. These small acts—the pleases, thank yous, pardon mes, and so on—signify respect for others' feelings. These acts show others that we can be trusted as interactants. If we signify respect in these little ways, we can probably be trusted not to act in ways that will damage others' feelings, especially their feelings about themselves. What this implies is that being emotionally responsive to others is necessary for getting anything done with other people.

We must also be emotionally responsive to others to protect our own feelings. Others can, if they wish, reject our identity claims (that is, they can refuse to accept us as the good people we claim to be) or treat us with disrespect. Of course, we can do the same things to others; we can, if we are so inclined, deny their identity claims and disrespect them. This is another way we are emotionally tied to others. We treat others respectfully not only so they can feel good about themselves, but also so they will feel obligated to treat us in a way that upholds our cherished identities and allows us our self-respect.

Most of our conformist behavior is based on our emotional responsiveness to and interdependence with others. In other words, our good or bad feelings about ourselves depend greatly on how others react to us and on how we imagine they are evaluating us. Consider, for example, the practice of leg shaving.

When I ask women in my gender class why they do such an odd thing, they usually say, "Oh that, well, that's just a personal choice; I do it because I think my legs look better shaved." This is a useful answer, because it is not at all mindful. To show this I ask, "Why is it, then, that every woman in the class makes this same choice? If it were really a personal choice, wouldn't there be at least 10 percent who chose differently, especially in a culture that supposedly values individuality?" After a minute, the answers come: "My boyfriend would hate it"; "People would think you are a lesbian"; "You couldn't wear shorts in public because people would stare." So what is really at stake are feelings about one's self, as affected by the real or imagined reactions of others.

You might think, "So what if our culture favors hairless legs on women and disfavors dresses on men? What's the big deal? Every culture has its fashions." This is true, but it is not the point, which has to do with why people feel compelled to conform to traditions. What is important to see is that the force of tradition arises in large part from our emotional responsiveness to others. This responsiveness arises, in turn, from our ability to imagine how others are judging us, and from a desire to feel good about ourselves. It is hard to feel good about ourselves if we imagine that others think we are stupid, ugly, or immoral.

The Risk of Cutting Ourselves Off from Others

Our emotional responsiveness to others gives us incentive to treat them with respect and to try to get along peacefully. Knowing that our feelings are in the hands of others, and their feelings are in ours, we have good reason to be kind and gentle with each other. It is possible, however, for our responsiveness to break down. Under some conditions we may cut ourselves off from feeling with and for certain others.

In war, for example, people in one country define those in another country as enemies. But that is not all. For war to be carried out, people in opposing countries must stop feeling with and for each other. This emotional cutting-off is what enables ordinary and otherwise decent people to kill in cold blood. If people on both sides could feel the anguish of those who were shot, cut, blinded, burned, and maimed, there could be no war. Politicians and generals who gave orders to kill might then be banished to a place where they could do no more harm.

Even in war people remain emotionally responsive to *some* others: fellow citizens and comrades in battle. In the face of a common enemy and the prospect of death, emotional bonding can be intense. If people lack this kind of intense connection in everyday life, they may find war attractive. It is as if the price of temporarily loving one's neighbor, or fellow soldier, is the mass killing of others.

Part of the problem is that we become too responsive to the judgments of some audiences and thus feel compelled to do things we know are not right. Our desires to be accepted and liked by people in one group can lead us to hurt people in other groups. Being sociologically mindful, we are alert to this danger. If we sense that our allegiance to one group is leading us to treat members of another group as less than human, we can ask ourselves, "What will the consequences be if I disregard the humanity of others just to be accepted here?" That is a question that should be posed aloud to other self-regulating humans.

People do not have to be at war for a cutting-off of emotional responsiveness to occur. If members of one group feel there is no way to gain respect from members of another group, members of the disrespected group may stop caring about the feelings and judgments of members of the other group. Often this kind of situation arises between dominant and oppressed groups. For example, in the United States, centuries of white disrespect for blacks has led to contempt for white people, and a disdain for things defined as "white," on the part of many black people. This is not "reverse racism," but rather a rejection of a dominant, disrespectful culture.

Not responding emotionally to others can thus be an act of self-defense. It may simply be too painful to care about the judgments and feelings of those who will not respect us in any case.

There are, however, other reasons why this cutting-off might occur. It may be that members of a dominant group feel shame and guilt at the suffering they have caused others. To listen to and feel with those who have been abused and deeply hurt may be too painful to bear. Perhaps this is why many whites in the United States have such a hard time listening to blacks describe the pain caused by racism. It is too much for whites to feel this pain and sadness, and to admit that they are partly responsible for causing it.

A similar thing can happen between people who love each other. If someone else hurts a person we love, we rush to be sympathetic and empathic. We try to feel with and for the person who is hurt. But if *our* actions are the source of the loved one's pain, we may be unresponsive emotionally. Perhaps we use reason to avoid dealing with feelings. We might say, "It's too bad that you feel hurt, but if you just think carefully about the situation, you will realize that you have mistakenly interpreted my actions; therefore you should not feel the way you do."

Few of us want to feel the guilt that comes with knowing that we have hurt a person we love, so we might try to define them as irrational, overly sensitive, or wrong about our intentions. Ironically, we do this because we *are* so emotionally responsive to others. If we were not, we would not have to be so clever in using reason to avoid the unpleasant feelings that can be induced in us by others' suffering. Sometimes it is our fear of how others can make us feel, if we open ourselves to feeling with and for them, that pushes us apart.

Reason is not the enemy of emotion. Reason helps us sort through our feelings and choose the best course of action—perhaps the one that best respects the feelings of others. Precisely because we sometimes have impulses to lash out at others, we need reason to be peacefully self-regulating. I am using reason here, for example, to argue for the importance of being emotionally responsive to others. A problem arises only when we use reason to avoid listening to others when we don't know how to deal with their feelings or our own.

Mindful Resistance

All of us care more about some audiences than others. For all of us there is always some group that matters, whether we admit it or not. Even the teenager who strikes a pose and says, "I don't care what *anybody* thinks of me," is cultivating an image to impress peers and annoy parents. The claim not to care what anyone else thinks is part of the performance.

There may, however, be good reasons to resist the judgments of certain others. Women might decide not to shave their legs as a way to oppose a sexist culture that insists upon women being smooth and soft and pleasing to men. African Americans might decide not to straighten their hair as a way to resist a racist culture that imposes a Caucasian standard of beauty. We might all decide not to care about the judgments of politicians and generals who tell us that to be loyal citizens we must hate and kill people in another country. In cases such as these, deciding not to care about certain audiences can be a way to resist oppression.

It is a serious matter to decide not to care about the judgments and feelings of any group of people. There will be costs, of course. A woman who does not shave her legs may have to work harder to find a partner who shares her anti-sexist values. In some places, a person who resists the power of corporate bosses can face job loss, jail, torture, and death. So we must be mindful in our acts of resistance. If we decide to ignore the wishes and feelings of one group, it must be because doing so will help promote justice and equality in the larger human community.

If we are sociologically mindful, we can see that our emotional responsiveness to others is greatly affected by the conditions under which we live. For example, in a society where there is much suffering because of inequality and injustice, it may be hard to stay open to feeling with and for others. We might feel overwhelmed by all this distress and thus try to shut it out. It may also be hard to feel the distress of others if we are the victims of injustice and inequality ourselves and are thus eaten up with suffering of our own.

Inequality can affect emotional responsiveness in other ways. Members of powerful groups may be unresponsive to the powerless because power fosters a lack of regard for others' feelings. At the same time, members of oppressed groups may develop a defensive lack of regard for the feelings and judgments of the powerful, since it seems that respect cannot be earned in any case. And in extraordinary times, times of war, many people in a society may try to cut themselves off emotionally from those with whom they are fighting.

Perhaps you can see how the boundaries between groups are important. These boundaries determine who are the insiders—people like us—who deserve care and respect, and who are the outsiders—people who are different—who deserve less care and respect. Of course, we do not *have* to believe in such boundaries and the illusion of difference they create. Being sociologically mindful, we will question all boundaries and categories, since they can diminish our emotional responsiveness to others, thus making disrespect and abuse more likely.

Sociological mindfulness helps us see more than just the importance of socialization. Most of us know that producing kind, gentle, intelligent people requires careful nurturance. If we are sociologically mindful, we can see something more: How we organize ourselves to live together also affects the creation of human beings. A great deal of inequality in a society generates fear, abuse, distrust, disrespect, anger, and even hatred and cuts people off from each other. In such a society it is as if many of us grow up in boxes.

Being sociologically mindful, we will pay attention to how social life shapes us as human beings. We will ask, "Do our beliefs and our ways of living together aid or inhibit our ability to be peacefully self-regulating and emotionally responsive to others?" Sociological mindfulness is not an answer to that question, but rather the practice of seeking an answer—a practice that is crucial to seeing how we might create a better social world. By being sociologically mindful, we can see not only how we become human, but also how we might live more humanely.

RELATED READINGS

Erikson, Erik. (1950). *Childhood and Society*. New York: Norton.

Gerth, Hans, & Mills, C. Wright. (1964). *Character and Social Structure*. New York: Harbinger.

Goffman, Erving. (1967). *Interaction Ritual*. New York: Pantheon.

Lane, Harlan. (1977). *The Wild Boy of Aveyron*. Cambridge, MA: Harvard University Press.

Mead, George Herbert. (1934). *Mind, Self and Society*. Chicago: University of Chicago Press.

Piaget, Jean. (1954). *The Construction of Reality in the Child*. New York: Basic Books.

Polanyi, Michael. (1958). *Personal Knowledge*. London: Routledge.

Shibutani, Tamotsu. (1961). *Society and Personality*. Englewood Cliffs, NJ: Prentice-Hall.

■ ■ ■ ■ ■ ■ ■ ■ ■ ■ ■ ■

Behavior As a Product of Circumstance

After a lecture a speaker might ask, "Are there any questions? Is there anything you would like me to clarify?"—and there is silence. Everyone stares mutely. This is a curious situation, since it seems unlikely that even a dull talk would produce no reaction from conscious adults. So how do we explain the silence? Perhaps it is that people who go to lectures, in college or elsewhere, suffer from a disorder called hyperquietism.

It might seem unlikely that everyone in an audience would have the same trait. And your own experience might tell you that the idea of hyperquietism is silly. Even though you rarely ask a question after a talk, it is not because you are naturally quiet. After all, in other situations you can be boisterous and loud. But this just deepens the mystery. How come people who are sometimes boisterous and loud, people like yourself, *still* sit silently after a talk?

Being sociologically mindful, we would try to answer this question by looking at situations rather than personalities. We would try to determine the conditions under which people stay quiet, even when they have a lot on their minds. Perhaps we would find that people tend to sit quietly when they feel that they are being evaluated for their intelligence, are not participating in a discussion as equals, and feel that, by asking a question, they risk appearing foolish. We might also find that these conditions exist in most places where lectures are given.

The point is that people act in response to the situation they think they are in, on the basis of what they think is at stake for them in that situation. Such a simple idea would seem to be easy to apply. Yet we often fail to consider others' perceptions of the situation they are in. If another person behaves badly we might think, "That's awful! I would never do such a thing!" Perhaps not. But perhaps also we would be less quick to judge if we stopped to consider how the other person perceives his or her circumstances and choices.

Here is another example you might recognize. In March of 1964 a young woman named Catherine (Kitty) Genovese was stabbed to death in Queens, New York, while thirty-eight people watched from their apartments. No one intervened or called the police, even though they had plenty of time to do so. You might think that this was a rare case, that people would normally help a person being attacked. Unfortunately, there are many documented cases of bystanders failing to help in similar situations.

You might think, "If I had been there, I would have done something." Maybe so. Of course, the people who watched Kitty Genovese die probably would have said the same thing had they been told of some prior case in which others failed to help a woman being attacked. Yet when the occasion arose, they did nothing. Were they simply cowards?

It might make us feel good to suppose that cowardice underlies the failure to give help, because then we can imagine that we, as braver people, would do better. Cowardice is as bad an explanation, however, as hyperquietism was in the earlier example. Again, we must pay attention to the context to understand what people do or fail to do.

In the Genovese case, the context includes a society in which few of us know our neighbors very well. In a big city, or even in a suburb, we may live near people for years and know little about them. So it might not be clear, on some occasion, if we should stick our noses into their business. This is also a society in which there are many angry and violent people, from whom the police cannot protect us every hour of the day. So it is not unreasonable to fear "getting involved" and perhaps becoming victims ourselves.

Situations can also be confusing. It might not be clear that help is called for or wanted. If a man in ragged clothes is lying on the sidewalk and people are casually stepping over him, should you bend down to see if he needs help? If you see smoke coming from under the hood of a car stopped along a busy freeway and hundreds of cars are speeding past, should you go back and help? Or suppose you see a woman rush out of a bar and a man come out after her, grab her arm, and jerk her around. Is this an assault in progress, a quarrel between drunken lovers, or an attempt to stop a thief?

Even if we think help is called for, we often prefer to imagine that someone else will give it. Perhaps when you see a man on the sidewalk, a smoking car, or a quarreling couple, you think, "Why should I be the one to get involved? I'm busy right now. In fact, I'm running late. Besides, if there's a *serious* need for help, I'm sure *someone* will give it." Of course, if everyone thinks this way, no one will help.

Recognizing that situations can be ambiguous, that giving help can be risky, and that we may innocently rationalize a failure to give help is not to offer excuses. Excusing or blaming is not the point, which is, rather, to be mindful of how circumstances affect people's behavior. It is to try to understand why people do what they do, rather than to judge them for failing to do what we, as outsiders to a situation, imagine that we would do.

To understand people's behavior in context, we must grasp the facts of a situation: Who does what to whom, where, when, how, and under what conditions? If we can't answer these questions, we do not know enough to understand why people act as they do. We must also be mindful of how the situation appears to the people in it. We must try to see things through their eyes, a task that is made more difficult by prejudice.

For example, young African-American women, especially poor women in inner cities, are often accused of having babies so that they can collect welfare. These claims are usually made by people who know nothing about job prospects in inner cities; about racial discrimination; about what life is like for poor, African-American teenagers; or about how much money welfare actually provides. Despite this ignorance, accusers will boldly say, "They are irresponsible! They don't want to work! They would rather survive by having sex, having babies, and collecting government checks!"

Being sociologically mindful, we would ask, How many babies are being had by whom? What does the world look like to these young women and to the men who impregnate them? How do they think of sex and of birth control? What does it mean to them to be a mother or a father? What options do they perceive for making a living and earning respect in their communities? Are jobs available for everyone who wants to work? What does it cost to live in these places, and how much money does the average job provide? How much money does welfare provide? With good answers to these questions we might begin to understand what is going on.

It is also important to let people explain their own behavior. We might or might not accept their explanations at face value. But we should at least listen to how people explain their own behavior before presuming to judge them. If we have not listened, then perhaps we should keep quiet until we learn more.

It is much easier to rely on stereotypes and prejudices than it is to find out the facts about other people's lives. It can also make us feel good about ourselves to condemn what we see as others' misbehavior, rather than to see how the behavior we dislike grows out of circumstances beyond the control of individuals. Being mindful, we will resist the temptation to elevate ourselves at the expense of others. Certainly we want others to consider the circumstances that lead us to act as *we* do, especially when we fail to live as saints.

Cultural Context

Being sociologically mindful of context also means paying attention to culture—the beliefs, values, and practices that are shared and transmitted from one generation to the next among a group of people. Culture, too, has to be put in a larger context, since culture is a group's adaptation to the environment in which it exists. Beliefs and behaviors that might seem strange usually make sense when we consider the conditions under which a group is trying to survive.

If we take culture into account, we can appreciate how behavior that seems weird or wrong to outsiders is normal and proper to insiders. This is not to say that any behavior is okay, merely because it is some group's traditional way of doing things, or because it aids their survival. It is to say that we cannot *understand* what people do, and why, without considering what they have been taught to see as normal and correct in their world.

We must remember, too, that people do not choose the worlds into which they are born. If we are born into a world of calm and wealth, we might learn to get what we need simply by asking for it. If we are born into a world of scarcity, struggle, and despair, we might learn that our survival depends on being aggressive, even violent. The point is not to justify aggression and violence, but to say that understanding others' behavior in context requires understanding the nature of the world that has formed their survival habits.

Imagine growing up in a place where any sign of weakness made you prey to abuse. Imagine that your survival depended on swift retaliation for any threat to your dignity, especially in public. Now imagine that your first job is as a sales clerk. In this job you must put up with being bossed by your boss, teased by coworkers, and insulted by customers. Will you respond, day after day, with patience and good humor, or will you fall back on your old habits and one day give your boss, a coworker, or a customer a punch in the nose?

If you come from a different background, you might think, "All low-level jobs require putting up with some obnoxious people. You just have to bear it until you get into a better position." If you believe this, it is because you have learned different survival habits. Perhaps you have learned to mask your feelings and do what the boss says, so as to get along and prosper. This strategy pays off well in some worlds, but it doesn't work everywhere, and it has costs.

Suppose you have formed the habit of doing as you're told. Imagine that this habit has gotten you a nice job with a high salary. One day you realize that a product your company plans to make is defective in a way that will injure some of the people who use it. You argue that the product should be redesigned to be safer, but you are told, "That will raise production costs too much. We will make it as planned. If anyone gets hurt, insurance will cover it." So you rely on the habit that has helped you succeed: You do as you're told. Then, as you foresaw, some people are badly hurt by your company's product.

After all this is revealed to the public, outsiders say that you should have blown the whistle or quit your job in protest. You could have kept people from being hurt, but you didn't. Why? We could say that you are weak and irresponsible—like those women who supposedly have babies to collect welfare. Or we could try to understand your behavior in context.

We should be mindful of your options as you saw them. Did you think you would be fired if you protested any harder? Did you think you could find another job if you quit or were fired? Did you believe that your career would be ruined if you blew the whistle, because of how whistleblowers are treated by other employers? Perhaps you had children to think about. If you'd lost your job, how would you pay for their food, clothes, shelter, medicine, school, and so on? So perhaps you felt compelled, for their sake, to keep your mouth shut.

We should also be mindful of what your job meant to you. Perhaps, like most people in U.S. culture, you learned to stake your identity on your job, so losing your job would have been devastating to you. Or perhaps you were taught that the boss who gives orders, not the worker who carries them out, is responsible for the results. That is a dangerous belief, also common in U.S. society, but we can't blame you for inventing it and putting it in your head.

To understand your behavior in this example we would have to be mindful of several contexts at once: the firm in which you had little power; the family and friendship networks of which you were a part; and the competitive, individualistic society in which you reasonably feared for your ability to make a decent living. In light of these circumstances your behavior, though not admirable, would at least make sense.

Interactional Surprises

Being sociologically mindful does not lead to the view that "context determines behavior." There is a grain of truth in that phrase, but it is important to see that what happens in a situation is the result of people trying to figure out how to do something together—with no guarantee that things will turn out as anyone expects. We must pay attention, in other words, to how behavior arises, often unpredictably, out of interaction.

We must pay attention to interaction because people do not simply react to a context; they join with others to *create* a context and to figure out what kind of behavior it calls for. For example, suppose you are having coffee with friends. What exactly is going on in this situation? Is it flirtation, seduction, therapy, domination, education, arguing, gossiping, worship, scheming, competition, or theft of ideas? It could be any and all of these, depending on how the situation is defined and how the interaction unfolds.

Suppose that you and some friends are talking in a café. A great many things might happen, some of which no one could predict. Perhaps at some point two men walk by holding hands. Seeing this, Pat says, "Look at those faggots. I *hate* that." Everyone is surprised to hear this, since Pat has never before made such homophobic remarks. Then Robin says, sharply, "Maybe you say that because you wish you were as brave as they are." With this brief exchange, triggered by the two men walking past, the situation is altered. What will happen next? Depending on how the scene plays out, people's lives could be dramatically changed.

Many scenes in social life are fairly predictable. If you go to the store or to the movie, you have a pretty good idea of what will happen. Even so, things could happen that you don't expect. Perhaps the checkout clerk comments on your purchase of pickled herring and you end up in a conversation that leads to a date and a new relationship. At the movie the people behind you might throw popcorn in your hair—and then you end up getting in a fight and thrown in jail. Even in familiar situations we can never be completely sure what will happen.

Here is another example, in the form of a story about a young man, Thomas, who grew up in a public housing project in Chicago. He studied hard in school and won a scholarship to an Ivy League university. During spring break of his first year in college, while many of his friends went to Florida to play, Thomas visited his family. He knew that his mother could use help with the younger kids, if only for a week.

The night before he was supposed to go back east, Thomas got together with his old hanging buddies Derek and Jamal, neither of whom was in college. Although Thomas had been a good student and never got in any serious trouble, he was hardly an angel. After all, he had grown up in a tough area and had to be tough to survive. Jamal and Derek teased him about going to college to become a "fat, rich white man." Thomas accepted the teasing because he knew it was a way for his friends to vent some of their own frustrations.

Thomas, Derek, and Jamal joked and talked for hours. Now it was late and they'd all had a lot to drink. Thomas said he had to get going because his flight was early the next morning. As he and his friends walked home, a car full of slightly younger boys from a nearby housing project pulled up alongside them. Someone yelled from the car, "You muthafuckas better get your ass off our street." Derek yelled back, and the car accelerated, then turned at the next corner, half a block away.

The car kept going and after a tense minute Thomas and his friends began to joke about "kids these days" and who would've won if there'd been a fight. But the mood was spoiled, and Thomas and his friends now walked quietly and warily. In another block they came to the apartment building where Thomas's mother lived. Thomas and his friends stood on the sidewalk saying their good-byes when a car came speeding down the street. Four doors flew open before the car screeched to a halt in front of them. It was the same car as before.

Five boys poured out of the car and surrounded Thomas and his friends. Two of the boys were older and bigger than the others. One of the older boys said, "You muthafuckas need a lesson in respect." Jamal stepped up to the first boy and said, "There's gonna be a lesson, asshole, but you sure ain't the teacher." The first boy reached under his jacket and pulled out a gun that had been tucked into his pants. Jamal grabbed for it but was too slow and got shot in the stomach.

As Jamal fell to his knees another shot was fired and the first boy's head snapped back. Thomas dove away, rolled, and in the next instant found himself crouched behind a car with Derek. "Take this," Derek said, handing him the gun dropped by the first boy from the car. Derek had a gun of his own. Thomas didn't want the gun but his hand seemed to reach for it automatically. Two bullets hit the windshield of the car behind them and pellets of glass rained in the street.

The boys who started the fight were trying to get back to their car, which was still in the middle of the street with its doors open. Thomas heard a siren in the distance and hoped it meant the shooting would end soon. Just then Derek stood up and fired at a boy who was trying to get into the driver's seat of the car. The boy pivoted and fired back. Derek fell into the street, clutching his neck and groaning. Thomas wanted to reach out to his friend, but he felt as if he'd been paralyzed.

Instead of getting in the car, the boy who shot Derek began to walk toward him as he lay in the street. Thomas stared in horror. As the boy pointed his gun at Derek's head, Thomas stood up and screamed, "No!" The boy was so surprised that he fired into the pavement. He was still staring wide-eyed when Thomas shot him in the chest.

The car in the street sped away, and after what might have been one minute or ten, the police arrived. Thomas was in shock. He barely understood that he was being arrested for murder.

If these were real events, the story would not end here. Thomas's life has been changed. Even if he is not convicted of murder, it's doubtful that he will be able to resume his college life. What will happen to him? And though the story is over for the boys who were killed in the fight, we can wonder what will happen to their families and friends.

This story shows the power of context to catch us up in events and actions that we do not expect. Thomas and his friends just wanted to visit and have a good time. They weren't looking for trouble. If not for what the other boys started, Thomas and his friends would have gone back to their usual lives the next day. Thomas would have been back at school, in a very different and much safer social world.

You might think, "Yes, but Thomas and his friends should have known better than to be out drinking, in a bad neighborhood, late at night. And they should not have yelled back at the car in the first place." It is tempting to think this way. We often try to make sense of people's troubles by blaming individuals instead of thinking about the context.

Being mindful, however, we would try to see the situation through the eyes of Thomas and his friends. To them this was not a "bad neighborhood," but the place where they had grown up and where two of them still lived. Hanging out and walking down the street at night were things they had always done. They were also young men who had learned that it could be dangerous to let an insult go unanswered. You might say that yelling back was a bad choice this time, but that is hindsight. If the other boys hadn't pursued the fight, you would think that Thomas and his friends just did what was normal in their social world.

Or perhaps you think, "Thomas was smart, successful in school, and had everything going for him. He should have known better than to get into a fight." Again, that is easy to say as an outsider. Thomas didn't want to get in a fight, but he was caught up in a situation where his life and the lives of his friends were at stake. He could hardly say, "Wait a second guys, I'm a college boy on my way to a bright future. Leave me out of this." It is unrealistic to expect that sort of response, considering how Thomas grew up, his loyalty to his friends, his regard for his own honor, and the threat posed by the situation.

Being sociologically mindful, we can see that what happened to Thomas and his friends was not any one person's doing but a result of interaction. Everyone collaborated, so to speak, in making happen something that perhaps none of them really wanted. Events unfolded as they did because of how Thomas and his friends, and the other boys, perceived the demands of a situation that they had created together.

The story also suggests another way we need to be mindful of context. We need to look beyond the immediate situation and ask, Why did these young men have so little regard for their futures that they would get involved in deadly violence? Why didn't they all have good lives to look forward to? How did they come to think that violence was the proper way to prove they were men? And how did they happen to have such easy access to guns?

To ask such questions is to be mindful of the larger context within which the scenes of social life are played out. We must be mindful, in other words, not only of the action onstage, but also of how the props, the script, and the theater itself are created. Or, to hark back to chapter 3, we must be mindful of the connections between a scene and the context in which it occurs. If we do this, we will see patterns where before we saw random events. Perhaps then all the stories that are in some way like Thomas's will begin to make sense.

Minding and Un-minding the Self

If there is a football field near you, go there and tear down a goal post. If the cops try to stop you, tell them to get lost. Here are some other things you can do when you have the time: run naked down a busy sidewalk; go up to a car at a stoplight and begin rocking it as if you are going to tip it over; find an area where there are beautiful old oak trees and throw rolls of toilet paper up into the branches until the trees are streaming with the stuff. While you're doing these things, chant loudly, "We're number one! We're number one!"

You might think these are crazy things to do. If you did them right now, by yourself, you would probably be arrested and forced to undergo psychiatric testing. But if you wait until your football team wins a big game, and a few thousand other fans join you, you could probably do any of these things without getting locked up. Your behavior might be seen as a bit obnoxious, but it would not be seen as evidence of mental illness or evil intent. Most likely you would be seen as "getting a bit carried away."

Just to be clear about this: I do not think you should do any of these things at any time, since they are hurtful to other people and disrespectful to the earth. The point in bringing them up is to offer another example of how to be sociologically mindful of context and its influence on behavior.

The usually temperate person who goes wild in a crowd might say, afterward, "I don't know what came over me. I just didn't seem to care what happened. It was like it wasn't even me doing that stuff." These might seem like hollow excuses, but they are probably close to the truth. The self-awareness on which we depend to control our behavior can be greatly reduced in a crowd.

One reason we do not usually wreck property, befoul trees, and run naked in the street is that we can imagine how others would react to us if we did. Most of us prefer not to be seen as destructive and foolish. And so even if we sometimes have urges to do crazy and hurtful things, we do not usually act on those urges because we can imagine the trouble we would cause ourselves and others.

But in a crowd, people may feel anonymous. They may feel as if they won't be recognized and held accountable for their acts. When people "act crazy" in crowds and do things they would not normally do, it is because they have stopped caring, for a moment, about how they will be judged, at least by any audience that is important to them. Or we might say that wildness results because people feel there is no chance that they will be held accountable for their behavior by any audience whose disapproval matters.

Defining the Situation

You might think, "It is not merely a crowd that makes the difference, since people don't automatically go berserk in a crowd, and most crowds are not rowdy." You would be right, of course. What matters is not merely the presence of others but how a situation is defined. In the postgame situation, people want to bask in the reflected glory of their conquering heroes. It is a situation in which people are allowed, even encouraged, to show that they too possess the indomitable spirit of champions. How does one do this? Perhaps by ignoring the usual rules of public civility. Winners, after all, make their own rules.

Yet the same people who are rowdy after a football game will be solemn at a funeral. Again, what matters is how the situation is defined, which is to say, what matters is the idea that people share about what is supposed to be going on. People might feel anonymous in a funeral crowd, if the crowd is big enough. But they will probably not violate the mood of the occasion by dancing around the grave and singing, "Ding dong! The wicked witch is dead."

The presence of others can sometimes *raise* self-awareness. Perhaps you can sing "Amazing Grace" in beautiful resonant tones— in the shower. But suppose you were in a classroom and the teacher said, "Before we discuss the nature of the carbon bond in the benzene molecule, we will sing 'Amazing Grace' to help us get in the mood for learning." Would you sing boldly, or would you hold back?

You might worry about being exposed as a rotten singer. Or you might want others to see that you are too cool to do anything as silly as singing "Amazing Grace" in a chemistry class. Or, even if you had a sweet voice and *wanted* to sing, you might worry about singing louder than others and seeming to show off. In a situation like this, your self-awareness would be raised and you would probably try hard to control yourself.

Whether we feel anonymous and reckless or self-conscious and cautious depends on how a situation is defined. Is the situation one in which people expect to criticize each other for how well they perform, or one in which people expect to be free from others' scrutiny and judgments? Being sociologically mindful of why people act as they do in any given situation means paying attention to how the situation is defined and to the degree of self-awareness it induces. This isn't easy to do, especially from the outside of situations that are unfamiliar to us.

Seeing the Bigger Picture

When the arteries that supply blood to the heart get clogged with fat, part of the heart muscle is starved of oxygen and may be damaged. If the damage is severe, the heart may stop working entirely, thus causing death. While this is a true account of why people have heart attacks, it is awfully narrow. Heart attacks are not merely mechanical malfunctions.

Arteries get clogged largely because people eat badly and don't exercise. Arteries are also damaged by smoking. Certainly these behaviors must be taken into account to understand why people have heart attacks. Stress is another risk factor for heart trouble. That, too, must be considered. But even after we have taken all this into account, we must ask, "Why do people eat badly, get so little exercise, harm their bodies by smoking, and feel so stressed?" To answer these questions we would have to examine the social worlds in which people live.

This wider view of heart disease—a view that takes behavior and social context into account—is "holistic." In medicine, a holistic view helps us understand more fully the causes of disease. It helps us see that fighting disease and creating health may require changes in the environment, in behavior, and in cultural habits. The idea is to try to see the whole and how things within it are connected.

Being sociologically mindful and thinking holistically are much the same. Being sociologically mindful, we try to see the whole—that is, to see the larger contexts in which people act and cultural habits arise. To put it another way, it is a matter of looking at the bigger picture.

Consider again the postgame rampage. Why do people seek these situations that license them to get carried away? Perhaps it is because they resent the restrictions normally placed on them by parents, teachers, and bosses. People who feel such resentment may be eager to create occasions where they can run amok with impunity. So why is it, we should also ask, that in our society there are so many people trying to control us?

Historical Context

One time in class a white student said, "It seems to me that black people are racists among themselves. I mean, look at how they give higher status to those who have lighter skin." Some of the black students scowled at this. After a moment, one of the black students, a very dark-skinned man, said, "What Todd said is true, in a way, but he doesn't really know what he's talking about." Before Todd could respond, I broke in and asked the black student to elaborate. He began, "Well, he doesn't understand the difference between racism and colorism, and he's also ignorant of history."

Despite its tense beginning, the discussion that followed helped us to see the differences between prejudice, racism, and colorism. The understandings we reached were these. *Prejudice,* we said, refers to believing that people in certain groups are inferior or evil. In this sense, anyone can be prejudiced. *Racism,* on the other hand, refers to the beliefs and practices that a dominant group uses to keep another group of people down. Members of an oppressed group thus could be "prejudiced against" members of the dominant group, in the sense of seeing them all as evil, but it would be perverse to call this racism, since members of the oppressed group have no power to enforce their prejudices.

What, then, of *colorism* among African Americans? Why have light-skinned people (often those with one or more European ancestors) enjoyed higher status in the black community? Part of the answer lies in the belief, created and spread by Europeans, that light skin is more attractive than dark skin, and that light skin is a sign of superiority. This is a myth, of course. But the belief has been powerfully enforced—by the group with the power to enforce it—for centuries. So it is not surprising that members of the oppressed group would be affected by it.

Another part of the answer lies in the practice of whites giving extra privileges to Africans with light skin. Under slavery, such privileges might have included a job in the house, rather than in the field. Along with a house job came better clothes, better food, and, sometimes, a chance for education, friendship, and land ownership. What happened, in other words, is that some whites gave extra resources to those Africans who, because of their lighter skins, looked more European. These resources then gave lighter-skinned Africans advantages in striving for wealth and status in their own communities. Today we see the cumulative results of these advantages.

Perhaps you can see why this has created a complex problem having to do with skin color. Many light-skinned blacks are reluctant to admit that the advantages they enjoy today derive from a kind of skin-color collaboration with whites. And so light-skinned blacks have sometimes sought to justify their advantages over dark-skinned blacks by adopting the idea that light skin is a sign of better character. It is thus true that some African Americans have embraced a racist idea as a way to justify their own privileges.

Being sociologically mindful, we must put all this in context. Colorism in the United States was not invented by Africans; it is an artifact of racism, as invented and practiced by Europeans. Colorism arose because of the conditions under which Africans, brought to North America as slaves, struggled to survive and gain their freedom.

To understand why colorism arose and why it persists we must take this historical context into account. The lesson is that to understand the troubles that exist in any community, we must be mindful of how it is connected to the larger community that surrounds it.

Ordinary Insanity

Earlier I used the example of people running amok and how this might be understood in context. Perhaps this made it seem as if being mindful of context is useful mostly for explaining outrageous behavior. All behavior, however, even that which seems perfectly normal, must be understood in context. Being mindful of context can even lead us to reconsider what is outrageous and what is normal.

Suppose that instead of running amok, people carry on politely and calmly. What could be wrong with this? After all, isn't this what most of us are taught to do? Yes, and most of the time it is fine that we do. Unfortunately, we can get so used to being polite and calm that we fail to be outraged by horrific things going on around us. Nazi Germany is the most often cited twentieth-century example. Millions of people were killed in concentration camps while most Germans went about their business without protest. How can we understand this complacency?

In Germany, as in other nations, the government claimed the right to use violence to control people within its borders. The German government, like other governments, collected taxes and used this wealth to build the means to do violence (by creating police forces, armies, spying agencies, weapons, and so on). Germans relied on this government to protect them from outsiders, to keep internal order, and to give them a feeling of belonging to a special group. Before and during World War II, most German people thought their government was doing these jobs reasonably well, or at least not so badly as to inspire a mass revolt.

Think of the German government—its employees, the rules by which it worked, and the resources it possessed—as an instrument for doing the will of those who controlled it. When the Nazi leaders gained control of the German government, they gained control of an organization that was equipped with (or had the legitimacy to gather and employ) vast resources of people, information, money, and weapons. It would have been hard for unorganized dissenters to resist such an entity.

The German government was also highly bureaucratic. Like any such organization, it had many rules and policies and layers of management for keeping people under control. It was thus hard for people to challenge their bosses, or even to find out what was going on. If you have had much experience working in large bureaucratic organizations, you know the problem.

Even when people began to see what was going on, most felt powerless and afraid to do anything. People who worked in the government and military bureaucracies—people who morally opposed the mass murder that was going on in the concentration camps—could justify their failure to protest by saying, "I'm not killing anyone. I'm not pulling the trigger. I'm just doing my job." After the war, many of the Nazi leaders who were tried for crimes against humanity defended themselves by saying, "I was only following orders." If those who actually killed could invoke this defense, imagine how much easier it was for people far from the killing to do so.

Looking back, the Nazi regime seems monstrous and insane. We wonder how anyone could have supported it, directly or indirectly. But again, consider the context.

After losing World War I, many Germans had feelings of injured national pride. Many were also angry about the terms under which they were forced to surrender in World War I. The German economy was faltering (in the context of a global recession in the 1930s), and many people worried about their jobs and income. So it was that many people were angry, resentful, and insecure—and confused about who was to blame.

In this context, the Nazis offered appealing messages: Other nations were to blame for limiting Germany's ability to recover from World War I; Jews, communists, and homosexuals were to blame for weakening Germany from the inside; and Germans were a naturally superior people who, if given a fair chance, could again build a great nation. These messages reinflated national pride and gave people easy answers to resolve their fears and anxieties.

We should also remember that once the Nazis gained control of the German government, they gained great power to shape people's thoughts and feelings. They used the government to make and control the news, to spread propaganda, and to stifle dissent. Many German people were thus at the mercy of the Nazi government when it came to knowing what was going on in their country and in the world. As in any nation-state, the Nazi government in Germany was a powerful tool for creating social reality.

If you have stayed with me through this unpleasant example, you might be wondering what is the point of all this. Is it to show that we can, by taking context into account, understand why the German people got caught up in acts of great evil? Yes, that is part of it. The more important point, however, is not about Germany in the 1930s and 1940s. It is about how we live here and now. We must learn to be mindful of our own context.

We still live in a world of nation-states, none of which is truly democratic and all of which have governments that can be captured by those seeking power for their own benefit. The governments of these nation-states still use violence to resist serious threats to their authority. Most of these nation states are capitalist, which means that many people are likely to feel insecure about their jobs and income. There is also still plenty of racism to fuel scapegoating. Conditions thus remain ripe for holocausts to happen.

Perhaps you think, "All this is true, and so it is fortunate that we live in a country with a benevolent government." That is certainly a comforting illusion. Being sociologically mindful, however, we will try to look at matters in a larger context and consider how things appear to Iraqis, Vietnamese, Nicaraguans, Cubans, Chileans, Guatemalans, and the citizens of other countries that have been invaded, bombed by, or otherwise forced to obey the wishes of those who run the U.S. government. We might also want to consider the perspectives of Native Americans, who can tell us something about the benevolence of the U.S. government.

An Antidote to Ordinary Insanity

Being sociologically mindful, we can understand why, given the propaganda power of the state, many people believe that their government is benevolent. The leaders of most governments try to foster this sort of belief because it helps them hold onto power. If we are mindful—in the sense of taking different perspectives in an attempt to get a more accurate and complete picture of how the world works—we will be less susceptible to the illusions that are supposed to keep us polite and calm while horrors go on all around us.

Sociological mindfulness can also help us to beware of our own tendencies to resolve anger, frustration, and confusion by accepting easy answers. If we are mindful in this way, we are unlikely to be seduced by politicians and other would-be leaders who want us to blame our troubles on powerless people. Sociological mindfulness is a good antidote to this eagerness to find scapegoats. Being mindful, we are more likely to see that our troubles arise from the abuse of power by those who have it, not from the adaptations of those who don't.

Being sociologically mindful we try to see the big picture. We try to understand how people adapt to the conditions of their lives, how they perceive their circumstances and options, and how they respond to the presence, expectations, and actions of others. All this is part of being mindful of context. We can take an even more holistic view, however, and try to understand people's behavior in the context of a culture, a community, a society, a nation-state, a global economy, and the course of history. Seeing the connections between action and context—and the next larger context, and the next, and so on—is much of what it means to be sociologically mindful.

Mindfulness itself is part of any context. A context in which people are sociologically mindful is different from one in which they are not. When being mindful, people can perceive the causes and consequences of their actions more fully. This awareness can in turn change people's behavior, which can in turn create new contexts. Where mindfulness thrives, there will be less ignorance, fear, and suffering in which evil can take root.

RELATED READINGS

Arendt, Hannah. (1963). *Eichmann in Jerusalem: A Report on the Banality of Evil.* New York: Viking.

Bourgois, Phillipe. (1995). *In Search of Respect: Selling Crack in El Barrio.* New York: Cambridge University Press.

Jackall, Robert. (1988). *Moral Mazes.* New York: Oxford University Press.

Kelman, Herbert, & Hamilton, V. Lee. (1989). *Crimes of Obedience.* New Haven, CT: Yale University Press.

Lever, Janet. (1983). *Soccer Madness.* Chicago: University of Chicago Press.

MacLeod, Jay. (1995). *Ain't No Makin' It: Aspirations and Attainment in a Low-Income Neighborhood* (2nd ed.). Boulder, CO: Westview.

Milgram, Stanley. (1974). *Obedience to Authority.* New York: Harper & Row.

CHAPTER SEVEN

Seeing Patterns

I sometimes ask my students to read a story called "A Typical Date Rape." The story describes a situation in which heavy drinking, misplaced trust, poor communication, the subtle threat of violence, and a man's refusal to take "no" for an answer result in rape. One time a woman read the story in class and said, "There is no such thing as a typical date rape. Each case is unique." I disagreed.

I said that the man who wrote the story had studied many cases of date rape and that the story summed up what he had learned. This explanation didn't convince the student. She insisted that each case is unique. I said, "Yes, each case may be unique in its *details*, but many cases have common features." Another student then offered this: "I've done counseling at the women's center, and I can tell you that this story is very realistic. It fits the pattern that I've seen over and over."

As it turned out, the student who insisted that each case is unique admitted that she knew of only one other case—one that didn't quite fit the pattern described in the story. Because of this she thought that there were no patterns and that it was impossible to generalize. She was mistaken.

Part of being sociologically mindful is seeing that the social world works in patterned ways. Many of the patterns are easy to see. Millions of people get up in the morning, go to work for 8 hours, come home, eat, sleep, and then get up and do it again. That is one kind of pattern, which exists because many people do things together in the same way, over and again. In fact, that is what a pattern is: a regularity in the way the world works.

The story about date rape described a pattern, one that was harder to see. It required the study of many cases of date rape to bring the pattern to light. It often takes a lot of work to discover patterns in social life, because some kinds of events don't happen every day. If you were asked to describe a typical bank robbery, you would have to study quite a few cases to see what they had in common. Perhaps then you would see a pattern.

Some of the patterned ways in which the social world works are obvious; some are not. Being sociologically mindful means paying attention in a disciplined way, so that we can begin to see patterns that are not so obvious. To be "disciplined" in this sense is to stick to certain rules of procedure when trying to see what is going on in the world. If we pay attention carelessly, we will still see things going on, but many patterns will remain invisible to us.

For example, it would be possible to examine many date rapes, bank robberies, or other crimes and find no patterns. This might happen because we failed to get the same kinds of facts about each case, so we might fail to see what a lot of cases have in common. A good rule of procedure for paying attention might therefore be: "Always get the same facts about every case." To stick to this rule—when it would be easier to ignore it—is what it means to pay attention in a disciplined way.

In chapter 12 I will say more about rules for paying attention. Here I want to say more about why we should try to be mindful of patterns, and why it is important to be *sociologically* mindful of them.

One reason to be mindful of patterns is that if we want to change the world, we must be aware of the patterns that make the world what it is. If we would like to prevent rape, for example, it is helpful to know what conditions, thoughts, and actions typically lead to rape. This awareness can help us to see which conditions, thoughts, and actions we should try to change, so as to disrupt the pattern that produces rape.

We can apply this principle—the need to grasp the pattern that produces a particular result—to anything we might like to change. To stop the spread of a disease, for example, we must know how it is spread, and to find this out we must look for a pattern. Where do cases pop up? Among which people? What do these people have in common? Have they all been to the same place, engaged in the same activity, or eaten the same food? By answering these questions we can figure out what the pattern is and how to keep the disease from spreading.

Sometimes it's important to be aware of and to disrupt patterns in our own thoughts and behaviors. Imagine a person who always agrees to help other people with their projects. Helping others makes this person feel good, but too much helping keeps her from getting her own work done. Because she doesn't get her own work done, she feels like a failure and gets depressed. Suppose this happens over and again. If the person becomes aware of the pattern, perhaps she can change. All that might be necessary is learning to say "no" when the requests for help become too great.

Patterns Within Patterns

Sometimes larger patterns encompass smaller ones. Consider, for example, the problem of sexual harassment at work. The typical harasser is a man. In fact, almost all harassers are men, and almost all victims are women, so there is a clear pattern of men sexually harassing women. Does this mean that women never harass men? No. In a tiny percentage of cases women are the perpetrators.

Perhaps you think, "If women can be harassers and men the victims, that means you can't generalize about men being the villains all the time." That's true; men are not the villains *all* the time, but the pattern still exists: Most perpetrators are men (and even when men are the victims, the perpetrators are still usually other men). But if women can sometimes be perpetrators, then we need to look for a larger pattern. If we study actual cases, we find that women who harass are like men in one important way: They have power over others at work.

The larger pattern thus has to do with power. If we look only at the most obvious pattern (men harassing women) we might fail to see the importance of power. But if we also look at rare cases (women harassing men) we are forced to think about what else might be going on. What we would see—the commonality that reveals a larger pattern—is that harassment (of all kinds) is most likely to occur when one person has control over another person's fate.

To see a pattern is not to know why it exists. Why do some people repeatedly trap themselves in bad situations? Why are rates of disease higher among some groups than others? Why do some people abuse their power and exploit others? Such patterns might be easy to see but hard to explain. Often we must dig deeper to find out why things happen as they do.

To see patterns in how stars work, we must study them in the ways that physicists and astronomers do. To see patterns in how organisms work, we must study them in the ways that biologists do. To make sense of the social world—to see and explain the patterns that make the world what it is—we must study how people do things together, the meanings and arrangements they create, the ideas they embrace, and the cultural habits they form. Only by paying attention to these things can we see the patterns that matter in people's lives.

There is more to this than looking for typical cases. To identify a typical case of something is to discern one kind of pattern. Other kinds of patterns can be seen if we pay attention to the social world in different ways. Being sociologically mindful, we may discover that the world is patterned in many ways.

Patterns of Difference

One way to describe how the social world is patterned is to say, "The world is divided into groups of people, and often the people in these groups share characteristics that make them different from people in other groups." This is no great insight. We learn early in life that there are different kinds of people in the world. What we don't learn, usually, is how to be sociologically mindful of the differences between groups.

Again, it might not be easy to see these patterns of difference. Do people in the group called "women" live longer than people in the group called "men"? Perhaps you have seen or known many old men but few, if any, old women. You might thus believe that men live longer than women. Actually, on the average, they do not. Women, on the average, outlive men (in the United States) by about 7 years. You would see this pattern, however, only by paying attention in a systematic way.

We should bear in mind what is meant by "on the average." It does *not* mean that all women outlive all men, nor that there aren't some old men who outlive most women. To say that women outlive men by about 7 years, on the average, just means that more women than men live to an old age. We might not see this if we looked at just a few cases. But by looking at all cases (or at representative samples), the pattern becomes apparent.

Being sociologically mindful we will ask, How do groups in our society differ in important ways? Some groups have more money, more education, better health, more prestige, and longer lives than others—on the average. By looking at these average differences, we can see patterns that reveal how the social world works. Or perhaps it is better to say that looking at such patterns can give us a snapshot of the social world. We would also want to know how these group differences come about.

We should be mindful, too, that group differences are not mere abstractions. They are indexes to how the lives of people in one group differ from the lives of people in another. If, for example, white families have much higher income, on the average, than Hispanic and black families, this tells us, or should lead us to suspect, that people growing up in these groups might have different kinds of experiences.

Group averages don't tell us about individuals. Even if white families have more money, on the average, than black and Hispanic families, it is still true that many whites are poor while some blacks and Hispanics are rich. In each group there is a range of incomes and wealth, so those at the top of one group can be ahead of those at the bottom or middle of the other group. Still, the average difference remains, and this pattern tells us about the status and power of various groups, even if it doesn't tell us about the experiences of every person in each group.

Interpreting Group Differences

We might argue about the meaning of group differences. One person might think, "Yes, there is a pattern here; some groups have much less income and wealth, on the average, than other groups. But this is because people in those groups are inferior to people in those groups that have more income and wealth." Another person might look at the same pattern and see it as the result of racism, sexism, or economic exploitation. Merely documenting a pattern of differences between groups does not explain how it came about. To explain the pattern we must study who does what to whom, how, and under what conditions. Human action underlies every pattern, and we must be mindful of this action if we hope to explain the pattern.

It is important to be mindful of how we interpret group differences. A lack of sociological mindfulness can lead to interpretations that reinforce inequality. For example, on the average men are physically stronger than women. That is a clear pattern, the meaning of which is often distorted.

To see the distortion, we should remember, first, that the difference is just an average difference. Not every man is stronger than every woman. Some women are stronger than some men, and the strongest women may be stronger than most men. We should also remember that the average difference is a result not only of biology but also of culture. If men are encouraged to develop their strength and women are not, that will lead to a group difference. If we are mindful of these matters, the "strength gap" between women and men does not seem terribly significant.

Yet this gap is often interpreted like so: "On the average, men are stronger than women; therefore men are stronger than women." That interpretation is misleading, because it turns a group average into a claim about every member of the group. It is not true that "men are stronger than women," as if all men were stronger than all women.

Why would anyone make such a mistake in reasoning? Perhaps because of the value attached to bodily strength in our culture. Strength is usually seen as a desirable trait, especially for men. In addition, men have often cited strength as a reason for their domination of women. It is thus tempting, especially for men of average size and strength—men who could perhaps be handled like children by the strongest women—to turn an average difference into a claim about a universal difference between women and men.

The problem is not that men can't think straight about these matters. Once again there is a larger pattern here. Members of dominant groups often make the same kind of mistake. For example, whites, on the average, have higher IQ scores than blacks. Although many blacks have far higher IQ scores than many whites, the average difference between the two groups is often seen by whites as meaning that whites are smarter than blacks. To whites, especially those whose IQ scores are merely average, that is a comforting, though illogical, conclusion.

(Having raised the issue, I should explain that the small black-white difference in IQ scores—a difference that persists even when schooling and social class are taken into account—has nothing to do with innate capacity. The difference results from two things. One is that many questions on IQ tests subtly favor people who are steeped in middle-class Euro-American culture, and this puts black students at a disadvantage. The other reason for the difference is that anxiety aroused by the meaning of IQ tests can lead black students to do less than their best. If you were told that your score on a test was going to be used as a measure of your human worth, or the worth of your people, your performance would no doubt be impaired by anxiety. It is also necessary to be mindful of context. In a society free from racism, these problems of bias and test anxiety would not arise.)

To be sociologically mindful when considering differences between groups, we should ask, "Is there more variation *within* these groups than *between* them?" If the people within a group are more different from each other—with regard to some characteristic—than from people in another group, then the difference between the groups is probably not meaningful.

Suppose, for example, that we wanted to know whether the women or the men in the town of Greasy Lake are kinder. Some people might guess, based on hearsay, that the women are kinder than the men. But if we wanted to know for sure, and if we wanted to know how big the difference was, we would have to measure kindness. Perhaps we could ask people how many acts of kindness they performed in the past year (presuming we could agree on what counts as an "act of kindness"). Anyhow, let's say that we get all the women and men in town to take the "kindness test" so that we can calculate a Kindness Quotient (KQ) for everyone.

It should be easy now to tell who is kinder, because all we have to do is calculate the average KQ score for each group. Suppose we find that the average score for men is higher than that for women. It might thus seem that we have our answer: Men are kinder than women. Suppose, however, that KQ scores within the categories "women" and "men" vary greatly. In other words, in each category there is a wide range of scores, telling us that, when it comes to kindness, women can be very different from other women, and men can be very different from other men. Yet, because of the high scores of some men (who perhaps overrate their kindness), and the low scores of some women (who perhaps underrate theirs), it turns out that men as a group have a slightly higher average. Where does this leave us?

Being sociologically mindful, these results should tell us that we have been on a wild goose chase. If there is so much difference *within* the groups we are trying to compare, and relatively little difference *between* them, we should realize that the categories we began with—women and men—probably have nothing to with whether people are kind. (We need not reach such conclusions by eyeballing the KQ scores; there are statistical means to tell if the differences are significant.)

The Kindness Quotient example might seem silly, but it is not so different from what psychologists who have studied "gender differences in personality" have done for many years. Ironically, the overall conclusion of many such studies is that, when it comes to personality, women and men are more alike than different. Sociological mindfulness would thus suggest looking for more meaningful groupings, if one must look for group differences at all.

Trends and Tendencies

Some patterns are visible only over time. We can see them when we watch how the world changes. A change that is sustained over time—for example, the continuing increase in the human population—is a trend. To say that most new jobs created in the United States since the mid-1980s have been low-paying service jobs is to cite another trend. Part of being sociologically mindful is paying attention to such changes and wondering where they might lead.

As with other kinds of patterns, there can be trends within trends. For example, since 1800 the U.S. population has never declined or remained the same; it has always grown. That is the overall pattern. There have been times, however, when it has grown faster than others—for instance, in each decade following a war. We could thus say that there is a pattern within a pattern: overall growth, with periods of more rapid growth right after wars. Again, to make sense of the whole, it is important to look for patterns within patterns.

Tendencies are patterns of probability. For example, chances are that people born into working-class families will end up in working-class jobs themselves. Of course, this is only a tendency. Some children from working-class or poor families will become doctors, lawyers, and professors. It is even possible that children of parents who are professionals will become factory workers, truck drivers, or trash collectors. Even so, the usual pattern—the strongest tendency—is for people to end up in about the same social class as their parents.

To see tendencies we must watch closely, over time, to see what happens and how often. Smokers, for instance, develop lung cancer at about eleven times the rate for non-smokers. Men get about a 45–70 percent greater payoff (in terms of earnings) from their education than women do, depending on the degree attained. These kinds of tendencies, like the tendency for women to outlive men, can be found by looking at group differences.

Trends and tendencies can remain invisible if we do not look at what happens in enough cases, over a long enough period of time. Suppose you were the first person from a working-class family to go to college, and suppose that most of your friends in college are from similar backgrounds. It might thus seem wrong to say that children from working-class families tend to stay in the working class—after all, you and your friends are proof that class mobility is possible. Yes, but beating the odds doesn't mean that there are no odds.

To see the real tendencies, we would have to look at representative samples of children from working-class families, over a long period of time, to see what kinds of jobs they ended up in. Only by looking at the big picture would the true tendency become apparent. Being sociologically mindful, we would want to avoid the mistake of over-generalizing from personal experience and to wait until we had information about many cases before saying what the pattern really is.

The point of trying to see trends and tendencies is to get a better sense of how the world works—although, again, observing a trend or tendency is not the same as explaining it. Doing that requires study of who is doing what to whom, where, how, and why. Seeing the trend or tendency is a step toward figuring these things out. Once we have identified the trend or tendency, we can begin trying to discern the human actions that produce it. If we are not aware of the trend or tendency, we might not realize that there is any action for which to look.

By identifying trends and tendencies we can also get an idea of where we are going. What if corporations continue to "downsize" and put people out of work? What if there are fewer and fewer secure jobs for people? What if the gap between the rich and the poor continues to widen? What if our inner cities continue to decay? What if the earth's population continues to grow at its current rate? What if more and more people feel they have no control over their lives? Where will these trends lead? What new problems will arise?

Sociological mindfulness does not answer these questions, though it does help us see why they are important to ask, and it may help us get to better answers. Being sociologically mindful, we will see connections, we will see the social world being made by human action, and we will see how people's behavior is shaped by context. If we are mindful in these ways, we can arrive at a fuller understanding of the patterns in which we are caught up and that we might like to change.

Flight, Feathers, and Other Things That Go Together

Seeing patterns is often a matter of seeing what kinds of things tend to go together or happen together. One pattern in nature is for flight and feathers to go together. Any creature (larger than an insect) that flies is more likely to have feathers than fins or fur. Perhaps that doesn't seem like a useful pattern to know about. Here, then, is another: Any slithering legless creature with a triangular head is likely to be equipped with fangs and venom. Knowing about that pattern might save your life someday.

Creating knowledge about the world is largely a matter of discerning patterns. When we learn what tends to go with what, or what kinds of events tend to happen together, we begin to know what's going on. If we know the patterns by which the world operates, the world becomes a more predictable and controllable place. If we know the patterns, we can do better at avoiding or solving problems. If we know how things tend to happen, we can perhaps intervene and make them happen some other way.

Being sociologically mindful, however, we should recognize the difference between patterns in nature and patterns in the social world. Patterns in nature (e.g., the connection between flight and feathers) are not human inventions. Our ability to see those patterns is socially constructed, but the patterns themselves are simply there. Patterns in the social world are the results of beliefs and cultural habits—our invented ways of doing things together. As such, these patterns are changeable. If people thought and acted differently, the patterns would change.

For example, you probably know that income tends to increase along with education. Just as feathers tend to go with flight, money tends to go with degrees and credentials. This pattern, however, is not a law of nature. We could change our economy to pay people for working hard—no matter what kind of work they did—rather than paying them for getting degrees. Or we could pay people based on how much money they needed to care for themselves and their families. There are many possible arrangements—which is to say, we could create different patterns.

Relationships Among Variables

Some people will say that thinking sociologically is about chopping the social world into "variables" and then seeing how they are related. We could, for instance, measure income (dollars per year) and education (years of schooling) and see if they rise together or are related in some other way. Perhaps, after a certain point, more education produces no more income. If that is the pattern, it might be worth knowing about, especially if one is hoping that a Ph.D. will lead to a big salary.

We could also look for patterns using the Kindness Quotient. Perhaps education tends to increase kindness, so that college graduates have higher KQs, on the average, than high school dropouts. On the other hand, income might tend to decrease kindness. This would mean that the effect of education is canceled out because education also tends to increase income. If so, this would explain why people who have gone to college are no kinder than anyone else. All this is silly, of course. It is just a way to illustrate how some people look for patterns in the social world.

Being mindful of patterns in this way is not always silly. It is worth knowing, for example, if people in certain racial, ethnic, or gender groups are more likely to be unemployed, paid low wages, or mistreated in some way. Looking at differences in group averages is one way to discern such patterns. Looking at what goes with what, under what conditions, is another way to get at patterns. Seeing these patterns, if they are indeed there, is essential to understanding how the social world works. But it is not enough.

To know that one variable goes with another is a starting point. Once we see a pattern, we must try to see how it is produced. Why, for example, does income tend to increase as skin color gets lighter? That is a troubling pattern that ought to be explained. To explain it, we would have to look closely at who does what to whom, how, and under what conditions, such that people with darker skins are paid less, on the average. If we are sociologically mindful, we will pay attention to the people and actions that produce the patterns we see.

Patterns and Individual Lives

A satellite camera can show us that clouds and storms are patterned in ways that we can't see from the ground. Being sociologically mindful is like taking a satellite view of society. It means trying to see the patterns that are not evident as we muddle through from one situation to the next. Sociological mindfulness requires gaining altitude, so to speak, so that we can see the patterns of human action that swirl around us and in which we are caught up.

It is not easy to take this view. Usually we focus on our everyday problems. This is understandable, because these problems seem most pressing to us. We might also think that we have about as much chance of changing the social world as of changing the weather. So why bother with the big picture?

Being sociologically mindful, however, we will see that many of our daily struggles grow out of the larger patterns of human action in which we are caught up. If it is hard to achieve dignity, security, and peace in our lives, it is largely because we lack control over our workplaces, communities, and governments. If we are not mindful of how these patterned features of social life operate to diminish our control, we will never see how to change the conditions that keep generating many of the problems we face in everyday life.

One thing that is important to try to see when we look at patterns in social life is where we fit into them. Sometimes we are much like the typical case; sometimes we are right at the average; sometimes our lives play out according to the usual tendencies; sometimes we are at the center of the pattern. Other times we might be at odds with the pattern.

Perhaps our lives run against the grain. If so, we should try to understand why. For example, I said earlier that children tend to end up in about the same social class as their parents. But suppose that's not true for you. Suppose you have experienced "upward mobility"—that is, you have (or are on your way to getting) a more prestigious and better-paying job than either of your parents. This seems to break the pattern. How can you make sense of this?

You might think, "My life is different because there is no usual tendency; every individual is unique." This would be incorrect. If 90 percent of the people born into any given social class end up in that same social class, that is hardly evidence of uniqueness. We can truthfully say that the *usual* tendency is for there to be little class mobility. So if 10 percent do achieve class mobility, that is just another interesting piece of the pattern. Perhaps you are part of that 10 percent.

What is important, in any case, is to be sociologically mindful about how your life fits or doesn't fit the usual pattern. If it fits, ask how and why this is so. What do you have in common with other people whose lives have unfolded like yours? What kinds of circumstances do you share with them? What sorts of problems and opportunities? Being sociologically mindful, you will try to see how common contexts have created similar lives for you and others, whether you are in the 90 percent or the 10 percent. You can thus make better sense of the overall pattern by seeing how it connects to your life. By doing so, you can also make better sense of your own life.

Sociological mindfulness does not imply that people's lives can be understood simply by knowing the categories they fall into. Being a white male born into a middle-class family does not mean that your experiences will be the same as for all white males born into middle-class families. Nor does it mean that you will have no experiences in common with people in other categories. Even so, by virtue of being in certain racial, ethnic, gender, and class categories, you are likely to have a lot of experiences in common with others in the same categories. You are also likely to get caught up in similar patterns.

Trying to determine who or what is a typical case, examining differences between groups, looking for trends and tendencies and for "what goes with what" are ways to see more about how the social world works. If we pay attention carefully, we will see large patterns and many smaller ones. Being sociologically mindful about our own lives, we will also try to see where we fit into these patterns. We may thus discover that many of our "personal" habits of thought and behavior are adaptations to the larger patterns of social life that carry us along, though we need not resign ourselves to being carried along. Being sociologically mindful of patterns in social life makes it possible to change them.

RELATED READINGS

Briggs, John, & Peat, F. David. (1989). *Turbulent Mirror*. New York: Harper & Row.

Epstein, Cynthia Fuchs. (1988). *Deceptive Distinctions: Sex, Gender, and the Social Order*. New Haven, CT: Yale University Press.

Gould, Stephen J. (1981). *The Mismeasure of Man*. New York: Norton.

Laszlo, Ervin. (1972). *The Systems View of the World*. New York: George Braziller.

Nisbett, Richard E., & Ross, Lee. (1980). *Human Inference*. Englewood Cliffs, NJ: Prentice-Hall.

Pagels, Heinz. (1988). *The Dreams of Reason*. New York: Bantam.

CHAPTER EIGHT

Contingency and Cause

What caused you to read this book? That might seem like an easy question, but in fact, it is so hard that you could never answer it fully. To do so you would have to say how you became able and willing to read this book. You would also have to say how reading, writing, and book publishing came to exist, how this particular book came to be, how you and I came to be, and how you and this book fell together. All that is more than you could explain.

In everyday life we don't have to give an account of the universe to explain why we read a book. Most people are satisfied if we say, "It looked interesting," or "It was assigned." Even so, if language and books, you and me, and the circumstances that brought this book into your hands had not come into existence, this moment would not be happening. Everything that led to your act of reading these words is part of what caused it. No one could ever identify all these causes, each of which has causes of its own.

Here is another question: What causes colds? You might say, "People catch what we call a 'cold' when their mucous membranes become infected with a rhinovirus." That answer is right, as far as it goes. The real situation, however, is more complicated.

For one thing, rhinoviruses don't always cause trouble. The immune system normally keeps them in check unless it is weakened for some reason. So we must think about what causes the immune system to weaken. We must also think about how the environment allows rhinoviruses to survive long enough to be transmitted and about what kind of behavior transmits them. A good explanation of why people catch colds would thus have to go beyond "bug gets into body, body comes down with cold."

Part of being sociologically mindful is recognizing that all explanations are incomplete. In trying to say what causes an event, a behavior, or a trend, we always face the impossibility of saying how all the enabling conditions came about. So we have no choice but to take most of these conditions for granted and settle for incomplete explanations of why things happen as they do. Such explanations are still useful, of course. You don't need to know how an engine works to know that if you turn the key it will (usually) cause the car to start.

In trying to make sense of the social world we often try to say what causes things to happen as they do. We don't usually care if our explanations are incomplete, as long as they make the world more predictable and controllable. Sometimes our explanations seem so good that we think we've found the One True Cause of an event. But this is an illusion. Events are not the result of a single cause but of a web of causes. Circumstances must come together in just the right way, at just the right time, to make things happen as they do. All events, in other words, are *contingent*, meaning that they are the result of a unique mix of circumstances and actions.

Perhaps the example of the 1991 Persian Gulf War can make this idea of contingency more concrete. Looking back, can we say what caused the Gulf War? Did it have one true cause? If you read about the war, you will find that each of these has been suggested as its primary cause:

- George Bush, then president of the United States, ordered the use of military force against Iraq because he wanted to raise his standing in the polls, distract attention from the nation's economic problems, make his place in history, and prove he was a man.

- The profits of U.S. oil corporations were threatened by Iraq's takeover of Kuwait, and so George Bush, acting on behalf of those corporations, used violence to put Saddam Hussein, the leader of Iraq, back in his place and restore U.S. control of the Middle East.

- Capitalists in developed countries profit by exploiting less-developed countries for their labor and raw materials, and so any attempts by these countries to get free from capitalist control cannot be tolerated; the United States thus crushed Iraq to show leaders of other less-developed countries what would happen if they got out of line.

- The Gulf War was fought to help justify the U.S. government's continuing huge expenditures on the military by showing that, even if the Soviet Union was no longer a serious threat, a strong military is still necessary to put down ruffians like Saddam Hussein.

Is one of these the true cause of the Gulf War? Each is plausible, and they are not incompatible; they could all be true. Perhaps you can think of other causes. What is important to see is that each of these explanations leaves much unsaid. Being sociologically mindful, we should pause to consider what is left out.

Nothing is said, for instance, about why the U.S. economy depends on imported oil; why people in the United States feel entitled to have access to the natural resources of other countries; why or how Saddam Hussein happened to have a well-equipped army at his disposal; why U.S. soldiers were willing to follow orders to kill people in another country; or why most U.S. citizens were willing to accept this violence being done by their government.

The Gulf War was *contingent upon* these conditions. If conditions had been different, the war could not have happened. We should thus be wary of any claims that the war had only one cause. The same principle applies to all events, large and small. Being sociologically mindful, we will avoid rushing to identify a single cause and instead try to see how events emerge out of a combination of circumstances and actions.

We can still try to determine if certain actions or conditions—like a virus getting into the body, an idea getting into minds, or weapons getting into the hands of soldiers—are necessary to make something happen. Even so, we must see that what ultimately happens depends on many other circumstances, some stable and some rapidly changing, coming together in just the right way. If we are mindful of how this swirl of contingencies can sometimes give rise to terrible events, we will pay attention to how things are shaping up at any given time.

Temporary Permanence

Perhaps I make it seem that social life is random and chaotic, as if every event is unique and surprising. Clearly that isn't true. Most of the time social life is orderly and predictable. You might think that this orderliness refutes the idea that events and actions always arise out of a swirl of contingencies. There is really no contradiction, however; the social world is both changing and stable at the same time.

Because human lives are short, we often mistake temporary stability for permanence. You might think this book, for example, will last a long time. Yet even now it is crumbling to dust, as are all the mountains and buildings of the world. The sun and earth might seem truly permanent; but in another four billion years the sun will burn out, collapse, and then explode to obliterate the earth before collapsing again. So even the planet on which we live is temporary.

Consider too that it takes work to keep the world orderly. If the sun didn't pump energy into the earth's atmosphere, all the plants and animals we know—including ourselves—would soon vanish. To keep the social world humming along from day to day, we have to put energy into forming and transmitting cultural habits. If we didn't do so, order would break down. The order we see in the world is thus not simply how things are or the result of inertia. Order and stability are the results of action.

So when circumstances shape up in just the right way to produce surprising change, it is always against the background of conditions that are relatively stable. In the case of the Gulf War, the background was an oil-hungry global economy dominated by a few powerful capitalist nations. Even though the war was brief, these background conditions existed before the war and still exist today. Being sociologically mindful, we remember not to take such conditions for granted, seeing them as part of the web of causes and the swirl of contingencies out of which emerges all that is predictable or surprising.

Being sociologically mindful means not only recognizing that our explanations are always incomplete, but also trying to see *how* they are selective and incomplete. Why do we choose to identify certain conditions as causes, while taking other conditions for granted? The answer lies in examining our preferences for seeing some things as extraordinary, while not seeing other things at all.

Reasons, Conditions, and the Possibility of Choice

If you throw a piece of chalk out the window and it falls to the ground, it would be reasonable to say that gravity caused it to fall. To understand why this happened, you might read a physics book. You would not ask the chalk to explain why it fell. On the other hand, if you threw yourself out of a window and fell to the ground, we would want to know why. Most people would not accept "gravity" for an answer, if you could answer at all.

Our actions are not caused by natural forces—the way that gravity causes chalk to fall. Does it make sense to say that heat causes people to go to the beach? Even though a lot of people might go to the beach when it gets hot, to say that the weather caused them to go would be silly. People can choose other ways to cool off. Or they can choose to do nothing at all. Chalk can't make choices, so it is fair to apply the language of causes to chalk and other inanimate objects. We should be wary, however, of applying this language to humans.

One time in class a student said, "I read in a textbook for another class that race causes criminal defendants to get longer sentences." He meant that black people who are convicted of crimes tend to get longer jail and prison sentences than whites who are convicted of similar crimes. He was right about the pattern; black people do tend to get longer sentences, on the average, for the same crimes, everything else being equal. But it was misleading, I said, to say that this pattern was "caused by race."

Being sociologically mindful, we would try to understand this pattern by looking at who is doing what to whom. Being sentenced to jail or prison is not something that just happens, like rain falling on one's head. Judges make decisions about these matters. So then we must ask, Why do judges give longer sentences to black people? Does race *cause* them to do it? Not really—no more than heat causes people to go to the beach.

As we all do, judges make decisions about people's character, and one sign of character upon which judges rely, perhaps unconsciously, is skin color. In our kind of racist society, African features are often taken as signs of bad character. Judges, most of whom are white, may thus decide that blacks need or deserve harsher punishment than whites. But it is not a defendant's race that causes a judge to see things this way. The problem, rather, is a body of racist beliefs that affect how judges think and choose to act.

We should not attribute the harsher sentences merely to ideas in judges' minds. Here, too, there is a web of causality. To explain the pattern of harsher sentencing we would have to know, for example, why judges feel pressure to appear tough; how images of black people have been shaped by the media; and why so many white people, not only judges, persist in seeing skin color as a sign of character. We should also keep in mind that, unlike gravity, all of these "social causes" are changeable.

Enabling Conditions

Another time, during a discussion about pornography, a student said, "I've read the chapter in the book and I can't tell if the author is saying that pornography causes sexual violence or not. Please just tell me if it does." This student wanted a yes-or-no answer and probably thought I was waffling when I refused to give one.

You can probably see why a statement such as "Pornography causes sexual violence" is wrong. Pornography is not a natural force that causes people to behave in any particular way. But if you are mindful of connections and context, and the web of causality, you can probably also see why it is wrong to say, "Pornography has nothing to do with sexual violence." Pornography indeed has something to do with sexual violence by men against women, but the connection is not simply cause and effect.

Sexual violence involves one person hurting another. For one person to inflict harm on another, the person doing the harm must disregard the feelings of the person being harmed. It is as if the injurer treats the other as an object—a thing with no feelings worthy of respect. How do some people's feelings come to be seen as unworthy of respect? This can happen only because some people create and spread the idea that other people's feelings don't matter.

Through words and pictures, pornography conveys ideas about women, ideas that can affect men's thinking about women. One idea conveyed by much pornography is that women are always ready and willing, despite outward appearances, to satisfy men's sexual desires. Another idea is that women are desirable because of their looks and their willingness to serve men sexually. A woman's thoughts and feelings, in other words, are less important than the shape of her breasts or her interest in having sex with men.

The ready *availability* of pornographic films and magazines (you could probably find them in a nearby grocery store) also conveys a message: It is okay to portray women as sex objects. If pornographic representations of women are everywhere, and there is little protest about this, then it can begin to seem natural and perfectly acceptable to view women as sex objects.

Do these ideas and their pervasiveness cause sexual violence? No, that is too simple a way to put it. Most men do not look at pornography and then feel compelled to commit sexual violence, even if they are aroused by the images. But this is not proof that pornography and sexual violence are unrelated. Being mindful about cause and contingency, we can see pornography and its ready availability as enabling conditions.

In our culture, young men are taught to believe that manhood is signified by having sex with women. So one way that men compete with each other—to see who is more of a man—is by trying to score sexual conquests. In this competition a man's goal is to get a woman to comply with his sexual wishes. Her feelings are worth considering only if they impede a man's sexual advances. A woman's feelings are thus not respected but are seen as problems for a man to overcome.

The larger context in which this competition for manhood status goes on ensures that most men will lose, because winning depends not only on sexual prowess but also on wealth and power, of which most men have little. As you might imagine, or as you might know from your own experience, these conditions can make many men feel angry and insecure. Now add pornography, which reinforces the ideas that women are sexual objects and that men know women's sexual desires better than women do. Under these conditions sexual coercion, in violent and subtle forms, is likely to occur. And often it does.

Being sociologically mindful about the "causes" of sexual violence, we arrive back at the idea of contingency. We have seen sexual violence as emerging from a conjunction of enabling conditions. So while we cannot say "pornography causes sexual violence," we can say that it helps create the conditions that enable and promote sexual violence. In this sense, pornography is one of a multitude of causes, a strand in the web.

If we are mindful about cause in this way, we can also see why abolishing pornography would not end sexual violence. One reason is that the ideas that promote sexual violence are not found only in pornography. And most of the other enabling conditions would not be changed by a ban on pornography. Then again, as some people argue, abolishing pornography might reduce sexual violence by making the ideas it conveys less readily available, and by making it clear that those ideas are harmful and should be rejected.

Reason and Choice

To raise the possibility of banning pornography brings us back to the matter of choice. Suppose that many people came to see pornography as a contributing cause of sexual violence. Suppose that many people came to see that using women's bodies to sell beer and cars and sporting events was also part of the problem. What then? Some people might say, "That's just how things are; there's nothing we can do about it." Others might say, "If these things cause problems, even if they are not the only causes, why accept them? If we have good reasons to get rid of them, let's do so."

To arrive at a sound opinion about whether we should abolish pornography or advertising that exploits women's bodies would require considering more issues than I have raised here. In any case, it would be incorrect to say, "There is nothing we can do; this is just how the world is; we must live with all the bad effects of pornography and sexist advertising." Being sociologically mindful, we see that enabling conditions can be changed. We can decide to do things differently and thus encourage different results.

Applying the language of cause to human behavior can lead us to forget that people act on ideas and meanings, and that people can rethink their ideas and meanings and choose to act differently. Of course, if people never question the ideas and meanings upon which they act, then they will keep acting in the same old ways. If people believe that skin color is a sign of character, then it might seem as if race causes discrimination. Being sociologically mindful, however, we see that humans create the ideas and conditions that sustain these patterns of behavior, patterns that mindfulness gives us the power to change.

Rules As Constructed Causes

If a teacher grades on a curve, giving A's to only the top 10 percent of the students in a class, does this grading scheme *cause* students in the top 10 percent of the class to get A's? You might say no, because the scheme is not a natural force; it is merely a chosen way of doing things. But the rule that says, "Only the top 10 percent get A's," has a kind of causal force because it always leads to certain results. No matter how hard students try, or how well the teacher teaches, only 10 percent will get A's. There is no way around this, as long as the 10-percent rule is followed.

The rules that guide a way of doing things together are like the rules of a game. As long as the rules are followed, certain results are inevitable. In tennis, for example, the rules ensure that no match ends in a tie; the rules of tennis always produce a winner and a loser. What's more, you can't win by jumping the net and tickling your opponent. That is not allowed.

Rules also produce unintended consequences. For instance, the rules of competitive sports ensure not only that there will be winners, but that most people will be losers and will suffer some feelings of anxiety and dejection. No one necessarily intends for this to happen, yet the logic of competitive sports makes it inevitable.

Part of being sociologically mindful is looking at the rules that govern social arrangements and asking what sorts of results those rules are bound to produce, regardless of people's intentions. We can do this with games, organizations, economies, and governments— with any patterned way of doing things together. All will operate according to some discernible rules and will, if the rules are followed, produce certain inevitable results. Capitalism is a good example.

A Life-and-Death Game

The most basic legal rule of capitalism is that a few people are allowed to control great wealth and property. If capitalists think they can make more money by shutting down a factory and putting thousands of people out of work, they have the legal right to do so. If capitalists think they can make more money in the long run by letting their property sit idle, they can let it sit, even if people are starving and could use the property to support themselves. The rule, in brief, is that property rights take priority over human needs.

Capitalism's other basic rule is this: To make the most profit, get as much work out of workers as possible, for the lowest possible wage. Paying workers less means that products can be sold for less, while still making a profit. A firm that pays its workers more will make less profit unless it can sell its products at a higher price. But raising prices usually means losing customers, who can pay less elsewhere. So a capitalist who doesn't drive workers hard and keep wages low is likely to go out of business. This isn't a matter of people being nice or not; it's just what capitalists must do to survive.

What happens when an economy operates by these rules? For one thing, there will always be inequality in wealth, since capitalists control the means to create vast wealth for themselves, while workers have only their time and energy to sell for a wage. Inequality will also tend to grow, although workers, if they are organized, can resist this. It is also likely that a great many people will be allowed to go without work, or with too little work to make a decent living, so that capitalists can control workers by threatening to replace them with more desperate people.

One time when I was talking about how capitalism works, a student (a business major) folded his arms across his chest and leaned back in his chair. "Are you saying that capitalism causes poverty?" he asked, with a mix of anger and skepticism in his voice. Before I could answer, he sat straight up and added, "It seems to me that capitalism *creates* jobs." This was a useful challenge.

Yes, capitalists create jobs, I said, but only if doing so will yield profits. If they did so for any other reason, they would not survive as capitalists. I said that capitalists will destroy any number of decent-paying jobs if they can replace them with low-wage jobs, because capitalists make more money when they can reduce the total amount they pay for labor. In fact, I said, capitalists create jobs only when necessary, try to pay as little as possible when they do, and try to get rid of jobs if they can, often by means of automation.

Much of what I said seemed to be familiar to this student from his business courses. But he was still unhappy with my way of putting things. He said, "Of course, businessmen try to make a profit, but that doesn't necessarily cause poverty." He was right. I said that even though capitalists had incentive to push wages down to the poverty level, that didn't mean they could always do it. Workers sometimes resist successfully; and sometimes workers with special skills can command high wages.

To get back to his point about poverty, I asked him, "So why is it that people will take such lousy jobs?" He said, "For one thing, people need to work, and then there are always people who don't have enough education to get anything better, or enough self-esteem to try." I said that his first point—about people needing to work—was very important. If people have no other way to survive, then we should not be surprised if they take whatever jobs they can get.

His point about education led me to propose a thought experiment. "Suppose," I said, "that everyone had a Ph.D. and high self-esteem. What then? Would everyone get a good job?" While he puzzled this out, another student said, "I don't think everybody could have a good job, because someone would still have to clean floors and pick up garbage and dig ditches. And even if people with Ph.D.'s were willing to do that, there probably still wouldn't be enough jobs for everybody. Look at how much unemployment there is now. There just aren't enough jobs to go around." The business major admitted that this was true.

"So, then," I asked, "why don't we use the government to create jobs for everyone, so that everyone who wants to work can have a decent job?" This time the business major answered: "Businessmen wouldn't like that." I said he was right, and that business*women* wouldn't like it, either. But why? Don't employers often criticize welfare and say that everyone should work? If so, why would they object to using the government to create jobs? He answered, "Well, I think it's like you said. If everybody knew they could get a decent job, they'd be a lot fussier and less willing to work at a crappy job for low pay. That would probably mean that employers would have to pay people more to keep them, and that would hurt profits." I was pleased that he was seeing these connections.

We still had not answered the question about poverty. "So does this mean that poverty is an inevitable result of how capitalism works?" I asked. No one spoke, so I rephrased the question. "If a capitalist economy can produce as much wealth as ours does, why does anyone have to be poor?" After a few moments a student said, "I don't think anyone would *have* to be poor; it's just a matter of how the wealth is distributed, and those who have it aren't going to give it up, at least not without a fight." Now we were getting somewhere.

"Where would the fight take place?" I asked. Another student said, "If you're talking about using the government to create jobs, then I suppose it would be a political fight." I asked who would win. We agreed that capitalists—those who benefited from conditions that forced people into lousy jobs—would probably win because they had more resources and more control over government. "Would they *necessarily* win?" I asked. The business major said, "Not necessarily. If workers in all industries got together, they could win. But it would take a huge fight."

We were running out of time, so I tried to sum things up. Capitalism tends to push working people toward poverty, I said, because profits depend on keeping wages low and even putting people out of work if machines can do the work more cheaply. Poverty also benefits capitalists because it means that many people will be desperate for jobs at any wage. Capitalists are thus in no hurry to end poverty. So while capitalism doesn't inevitably cause poverty, it does create incentives for capitalists to act in ways that make poverty a likely result, especially if workers are too disorganized to fight back.

The point of telling this is not to show that capitalism is all bad, but that certain bad results—inequality, lousy jobs, unemployment, poverty—stem from the way that capitalism works. If we think of capitalism as a kind of game, one that is played for high stakes and for keeps, we see that its rules make some bad results inevitable and others extremely likely. Once people are locked into the game, these results are bound to come about unless people change or break the rules.

Avoiding Reductionism

The rules that underlie social arrangements are seldom spelled out like the Ten Commandments. They are more like a hidden logic that has to be discovered. But once we see what the rules are, we can consider their consequences. It is like saying, "If we do things together in this way, if we follow these rules, where will it lead? What sorts of results will we create for ourselves?" These are just the first questions, of course. Being sociologically mindful, we would also ask who makes the rules and who benefits from them.

Being mindful about rules as causes can also help us avoid trying to explain social life in psychological ways, a mistake called "reductionism." For example, if someone said that football was violent because football players have personalities that make them prone to violence, that would be reductionistic. Football is violent because of the rules of the game. It can be more or less violent, depending on how hard it is played, but the basic rules of football require people to slam into each other.

A lack of sociological mindfulness leads many people to fall into reductionist thinking. For example, many people believe that poverty is caused by a personality trait called "laziness." When millions of people are poor even though they work hard at jobs that don't pay decent wages, then it is wrong to attribute the problem to character flaws. If we are sociologically mindful, we will pay attention to the rules of the game in which people are caught. In this case we should be able to see that the problem is not lazy or greedy individuals, but rules that cause people to treat each other as tools for profit-making rather than as human beings.

Chance, Pattern, and Paths

To say that people are "caught in the rules of a game" might make it seem as if the paths of people's lives are set by these rules. Not exactly. Even in sports, the rules say only how a game should be played; they do not say what will happen in the game or how it will turn out. There can always be surprises. No matter how many spoken and unspoken rules there might be, social life remains a swirl of contingencies out of which can emerge events that no one expects.

We see this when we watch people's lives unfold. No matter how much we know about a person's background, we can still be wrong when we guess how that person's life will turn out. But this doesn't mean that it's all a matter of chance. In people's lives, as in social life more generally, there is both chance and pattern. Being sociologically mindful, we will try to see how chance and pattern are linked. Perhaps the best way to show this is with a story that has two endings, either of which could be true. Here is the story.

■ ■ ■

Moira needed an elective. A friend told her to take Professor Valkyrie, but Moira had no interest in philosophy. "Besides," Moira said, "I can barely make sense of what's going on in English 212. I'd be way over my head in philosophy." Her friend said, "Yeah, I expected philosophy to be either totally boring or impossible to understand—you know, like Plato and stuff. But Valkyrie's great. She really makes you think. You ought to try her." When it came time to register, the astronomy class that Moira wanted was full. The only class that fit her schedule was Introduction to Philosophy, taught by Professor Valkyrie.

Moira's friend was right. Professor Valkyrie was good. She could explain complex ideas in a way that made them understandable. She also tied philosophy back to problems in everyday life. Moira liked this and found that it was helping her make sense of a lot of things. Moira worked hard in the course and impressed Professor Valkyrie. At the end of the semester Valkyrie wrote on Moira's final paper, "You've come a long way. Your writing and thinking are first-rate. If you ever need a letter of recommendation, let me know."

A few weeks later, after the spring semester had ended, Professor Valkyrie was going to lunch when she ran into a professor from another department. They decided to try The Penny University, a new café near campus. The food, as it turned out, was okay, but the service was slow and the cappuccino wasn't hot enough. It was as if no one had taught the people behind the counter how to do their jobs.

As they walked back to campus, the other professor said to Valkyrie, "The service at that place reminds me that my research assistant has got to go. He's screwed up too many times. I need someone more dependable, but I don't know where I'm going to find anyone during the summer." Professor Valkyrie said she knew a student who was sharp and might still need a job. When they got back to campus, they looked up Moira's number in the phone book.

The other professor called Moira, who said she was willing to quit at GrabnGo if the research assistant job worked out. They arranged for Moira to come in the next morning at 9:00 for an interview. Moira was excited about the prospect of better pay and more interesting work, but she was nervous, too. Even though she'd done well in Professor Valkyrie's course, Moira wasn't sure she was smart enough to do research.

Moira wore what she thought of as sensible clothes—nice, but not too fancy. She didn't want to give the impression that she cared more about clothes than about books and ideas. And even though she'd had to clean up her roommate's dishes before she could eat breakfast,

Moira left in plenty of time to be on campus by 8:30. She certainly didn't want to be late for a job interview.

About three blocks from her apartment, Moira was starting to make a right turn when a bird flew into her windshield. There was a splash of blue feathers and Moira jerked the steering wheel slightly, enough to cause the right rear tire to bounce over the curb. She stopped the car and stared at the spot on the windshield where the bird had hit. Moira felt sad, as if she had just intervened in the bird's life, only to destroy it. A car honked and Moira realized she was blocking traffic. "It wasn't my fault," she thought, taking a deep breath, "these things just happen. I'd better get going or I'll be late."

Moira had gone only another block when she heard a flap-flap-flap sound coming from the back of the car. The tire that had hit the curb was flat. "Shit!" Moira hissed to the inside of the car, checking her watch and pounding the steering wheel with her fist. She found a spot to pull over and quickly got to work changing the tire. As Moira jacked up the car, she kept seeing the bird hit the windshield. Now it made her angry, as if the bird had intervened in her life, knocking her off course.

Changing the tire left Moira dirty and sweaty. She knew she would be late for the interview and would be a mess when she got there. Moira called the professor from a burger place and told her what had happened. The professor said, "I see. Well, look, I've got another person I'm talking to about this job and I need to hire someone today. So I'll call you if I still need someone tomorrow." That was the last Moira heard from her. Later, when Professor Valkyrie asked the other professor what had happened with Moira, she said, "We arranged an interview but she didn't show. She called and gave me a flat-tire story. And frankly, I'd had enough of those sorts of excuses from the guy I fired. So I found somebody else."

Moira was disappointed about not even getting a shot at the job. She could tell that the professor didn't believe her about the flat tire. For a moment she fantasized about rolling the damaged tire into the professor's office and saying, "Here's the tire I told you about. I wrote my phone number on it in case you ever want to call me about another job." But all Moira could do was to go back to work at GrabnGo and try to save money for school.

Later that summer the assistant manager left and Moira was asked if she wanted the job. She wasn't sure. Moira had hoped to get her degree and a professional job of some kind. But with the exception of Professor Valkyrie's course, she hadn't exactly been taking college by storm, and she was tired of being broke. So she decided to take a year off from school and give the job a try. Moira figured that if she hated it, she could always quit and go back to school in the spring.

Moira found that she liked running the store. It was a challenge, at first, to learn how to do inventory, order stock, schedule maintenance, and keep track of payroll. Doing all this gave Moira a sense of competence. The hardest part of the job was not the job at all, but the loneliness she felt. She missed her friends from college.

That fall Moira started dating a guy who delivered beer to the store. At first she didn't want to get serious, but one thing led to another, and by January they were living together. After some adjustment, the arrangement seemed to suit them fine. A few months later, Moira and her partner were vacationing in Virginia. One morning, while feeling very much in love, they decided to get married—and they did, that afternoon.

Soon after they got back from the trip, Moira was offered the job of manager at a GrabnGo store in another part of town. By now Moira had found a new circle of friends and was thinking less and less about going back to school. "Why bother?" she thought, since she could make what seemed like good money as a GrabnGo manager. Her new husband had never liked the college idea, either.

Moira ran a good store and hoped to become a regional manager for the company. But three times she was passed over for promotions. Twice the jobs went to men who were a few years older and had degrees. Moira didn't see why a degree was necessary, but she didn't think it was unfair if someone with a degree edged her out—if everything else was equal. A year later, a slightly younger man who had been with the company less time than she had, and who didn't have a degree, was promoted to regional manager. Moira began to wonder what was going on.

After four years as a store manager, Moira was bored. She had learned all there was to know about running a GrabnGo store. So when she found out she was pregnant, it wasn't that hard to decide to quit and stay home to raise the child. Moira thought she would have one more child after that, and then, after both were grown, maybe go back to college.

That is one ending to the story. Here is another.

Moira was locking the front door behind her when she felt a flash of panic. Had she turned off the stove? She opened the door and went back in to check. Of course it was off. She had never forgotten to turn off the stove. But whenever she felt nervous about something, she imagined leaving it on and being blamed for burning the house down. "Maybe I should stick to cold cereal in the morning," Moira thought, as she spun around and headed to her interview.

About three blocks from her apartment, as Moira was turning a corner, a bluebird darted in front of her windshield. It came so close that she could see it was carrying a piece of straw in its beak. Then she remembered one of her grandmother's old sayings, "If the first bird you see in the morning is blue, you'll have good luck that day." Moira smiled and relaxed a bit as that thought crossed her mind. "Thanks, Grandma," she said out loud, feeling sure she hadn't seen any other birds that morning.

Moira found a parking spot near the professor's building. She sat on a bench outside the building for a few minutes, then went in and climbed the stairs to the third floor. Moira was still ten minutes early and was reading cartoons on office doors when a tall, dark-skinned woman with braided hair came down the hall. She was carrying a leather shoulder bag and wearing jeans and a gold vest over a white T-shirt. Her round wire-rimmed glasses matched the vest. "You must be Moira," the woman said. "I'm Professor Sesheta. Come in and have a seat. Would you like some coffee?"

The interview went well. Moira liked the professor, who was not what Moira had expected. When Moira asked what the job entailed, the professor pointed to a table in the corner of her office. It was piled two feet high with manuscripts and old newspapers. "The first task would be to go through that mess and create a bibliographic database," the professor said. "It isn't hard, once you get the hang of it, but you have to be careful and precise."

Moira admitted that, other than writing papers for classes, she had no experience doing this sort of thing. After talking for about an hour, the professor surprised Moira again when she asked, "When can you start?"

Moira gave her notice at GrabnGo and started working for the professor the next week. In a way, the work was easy. All Moira had to do was to put the title, author, and source of each manuscript or newspaper story into a computer program. Once Moira learned how to use the computer, the work went fast. But there were times when information was missing and Moira had to track it down in the library. She liked doing this sort of detective work.

It took about a month to get through the stack of manuscripts and newspapers in the professor's office. Then there were more manuscripts to go through in a special part of the library, a room in the basement where few people ever went. Moira liked taking the laptop down there and doing her work. It was quiet and meditative, and time passed quickly. Moira would also sometimes pause to read part of a manuscript. She seemed to be learning a lot without really trying.

Moira also talked with the professor about her research. The professor explained what her project was about and how she had gotten interested in it. Moira would sometimes ask about things she read in the manuscripts. These were the talks Moira enjoyed most, even though she didn't quite grasp everything the professor said. What was most satisfying, Moira felt, was that when she asked the professor about the meaning of something she'd read, the professor would give a careful answer that tied everything together. Moira wished her classes during the semester were like this.

Summer was over too soon, although Moira felt that a lot had changed for her in that brief time. School felt different somehow. Before, Moira had seen her classes as dreary ordeals to be endured on her way to a job and a real grown-up life. Now she felt that there was something to be gotten out of every class, and that it was up to her to go after it and not let a dull professor or textbook get in the way. It was both exciting and frustrating to realize that the world was a more interesting and complicated place than she would have time to fully explore.

A few weeks into the fall semester Moira ran into Professor Valkyrie. "Did you have a good summer?" Valkyrie asked.

"It was great," Moira said. "I worked for Professor Sesheta, mostly doing archiving and bibliographic work. The money was good, and I learned a lot."

"So does this mean you're not going to major in philosophy?" Valkyrie asked, half-teasingly. Moira laughed.

"Well, I had been majoring in 'undecided,' but now I'm leaning toward history. When I register for the spring I'll probably declare a history major with a philosophy minor. I want to come by and talk to you about that," Moira said.

"Come by any Tuesday or Thursday afternoon," Valkyrie said. "I have office hours from three to four."

As it turned out, Moira decided to major in both history and political science. It took her an extra year to finish the double major, but she wasn't in a hurry. She knew that she'd never again be so free to pursue her interests. Moira was also absorbed in work she was doing for a student group that helped the university's janitorial staff fight for higher wages. When Moira had learned that the university paid its full-time cleanup people a wage that kept them below the poverty level, she was outraged. She decided that before she left school, she'd at least try to change that situation.

By the start of her fifth year Moira knew she wanted to go to law school. Some of her professors suggested graduate school, but Moira didn't want to play academic games while there was so much that needed to be changed in the world. Her experience with the housekeepers had opened her eyes to other situations where powerless people were exploited. Moira felt she could do more to fight these injustices as a lawyer than as a professor. After three years of law school Moira got a job with a firm that represents unions, consumer groups, and activist organizations. Moira made partner after she won a big sex-discrimination suit against GrabnGo Corporation.

■ ■ ■

The two endings to this story show how people are caught up in a swirl of contingencies in which small events—like a bird hitting a windshield—can cause their lives to turn out differently. We can also see from these stories that it is not the small event alone that causes things to turn out as they do; it is a whole set of circumstances that come together just so. Even a small change in circumstances can bump a life onto a path that leads to a very different place.

Perhaps this makes it seem as if it is pointless to be sociologically mindful about individual lives, since each life unfolds as the result of a unique series of random events. If so, why bother to think analytically about individual lives? What sense can we hope to make of randomness? Lives are not really random, however, even if the swirl of contingencies makes their outcome unpredictable.

Moira's life was not random. It was part of a pattern. To see this, consider that there are millions of Moiras: young women who try to get ahead by going to college, but who must face conflicting demands from people in their lives, demands that arise because of cultural ideas about work, gender, marriage, and so on. The circumstances these women face are similar in many ways, and these circumstances make some results more likely than others. Even though the swirl of contingencies can produce surprises, like Moira becoming a lawyer, we are *surprised* only because there is a departure from what *usually* happens.

You can see this with Moira's story if you rewrite it. What if Moira's father had been a surgeon and her mother a university president? Would she have been working at GrabnGo trying to scrape together money for school? Not likely. Would she have seen a beer-delivery man as partner material? Probably not. Or what if Moira had been male? Perhaps he would have been promoted to regional manager and had a long career with GrabnGo Corporation. Any of these changes might have gotten Moira caught up in a different pattern.

Imagine flicking the tip of a twig into a stream. It is possible that a fish will mistake the twig for an insect and will swallow it. It is possible that an eagle will snatch the fish out of the water and eat it, twig and all. It is possible that the twig, a bit worse for the wear, will end up on the forest floor miles above the spot where you threw it into the stream. All this could happen. But what is most likely is that the twig will float downstream for a while, become waterlogged, sink, get stuck under a deadfall or against a bank, and decay. That is what happens to most twigs, because of how the natural world works.

Moira's life, like everyone's life, fell into a swirling stream of time and events. Yet the swirling, for all the surprises it might produce, is not random but patterned, as we can see if we are sociologically mindful. We can think of these patterns—and where we step into them—as what cause us to be pushed and pulled, like twigs in a stream, more strongly toward some places than others. We can think of the swirling, the ever-changing mix of circumstances, as what sometimes pops us out of one pattern into another, or toward unlikely places.

RELATED READINGS

Becker, Howard S. (1994). "Foi Por Acaso: Conceptualizing Coincidence." *Sociological Quarterly* 35:183–194.

Bloor, David. (1976). *Knowledge and Social Imagery.* London: Routledge and Kegan Paul.

Brown, Robert. (1963). *Explanation in Social Science.* Chicago: Aldine.

Campbell, Jeremy. (1982). *Grammatical Man.* New York: Simon and Schuster.

Davidson, Donald. (1963). "Actions, Reasons and Causes." *Journal of Philosophy* 60:685–700.

Toulmin, Stephen E. (1972). *Human Understanding.* Princeton, NJ: Princeton University Press.

von Wright, Georg Henrik. (1971). *Explanation and Understanding.* Ithaca, NY: Cornell University Press.

CHAPTER NINE

Images, Representations, and Accounts

The old saying "Do not judge a book by its cover" reminds us that appearances can be deceiving. What seems true at first glance can turn out to be quite wrong. Yet we judge books, people, and other things by their covers all the time. We look to see what we can see— the design of a book jacket, the clothes a person wears, the rust on a car's bumper—and make inferences about the qualities underneath. Why do we do this if we know it is so risky and can lead us astray?

One reason we rely on appearances is that we need to know what to expect from people and things. When we meet an unfamiliar person, we might wonder if s/he is friendly or dangerous, trustworthy or devious. We might wonder if s/he can give us help or will try to get something from us. Until we get to know a person we can't be sure about these matters. But still we need to have an idea of what a person is like, so we must make judgments based on the signs of character we can detect.

Another reason we rely on appearances is that we deal with many people whom we will never get to know very well. Many of our encounters with others are brief, and many people we see only once. Yet we still must determine how others are likely to act toward us— and thus how we should act toward them. To get along, we must learn to "read" others quickly. We do make mistakes, of course. We are most likely to misjudge a person's character when a stereotype interferes with a careful reading of the person as an individual.

Being sociologically mindful does not mean that we overcome the need to make judgments about others based on limited information. If we all lived in small villages, where everyone got to know everyone else very well over many years, then things would be different. But in a society like ours, we are forced to rely on what we can see and interpret quickly. Being sociologically mindful means being aware that we are doing this, being aware of *how* we are doing it, and being aware that all around us appearances are being crafted to influence our thoughts and feelings.

The social world is full of strategically crafted images and representations. To say that they are "strategically crafted" means that they are made with the aim of creating a particular impression. Consider the images you craft for yourself. On a job interview, for example, you must craft an image of yourself as capable and enthusiastic—all the while appearing natural, so that you don't come off as phony. On a first date you will probably try to craft an image of yourself so that the other person will see the most attractive side of who you are. It works both ways, of course; others are crafting images for you, too.

Perhaps this makes social life seem like a game of deception. You might think, "So, then, being sociologically mindful means seeing that everyone is a fraud, since everyone is trying to con everyone else with these bogus images." That is not really what sociological mindfulness leads us to see. Not everyone is a fraud, nor are all images crafted to mislead others. The point is that whether we seek to mislead or to reveal our truest selves, we must still craft images.

Suppose you want to express your love for another person. How can you do this? You must put your feelings into actions that the other person will interpret as signs of love. This is all you can do, since the other person can't look inside your skull to check for a feeling labeled "love." The other person must make an inference about your feelings, based on what you say and do. This means that you must craft an image that the other person will see as revealing your true feelings. Whether we are faking or being as honest as we can be, there is no getting around our reliance on images.

To use a workplace example again: It is good to be competent when you are seeking to be hired and promoted, but it is even more important to *appear* competent, because decisions about your future will be based on what powerful others perceive you to be. If you are competent and fail to create the impression of competence in others' minds, you will not do well. Then again, a person who puts more effort into creating an image of competence than into developing real competence may also fail when a crucial test arises.

The images we create are tremendously consequential. Our lives can depend on them. Others decide how to treat us, and we decide how to treat them, based on appearances. When we do this, we are not thinking, "I will rely on appearances to judge this person." What we do, more or less by habit, is to look for signs of people's inner qualities. The signs we rely on are those we have learned to see and interpret.

A curious result of this reliance on images is that we *create each other* in interaction. For example, you have probably been in situations where you felt as if you said and did everything right—and where you thus created an image of yourself as witty, charming, and good-natured. In that situation, that is what you were; from your performance, others could infer that you were indeed a witty, charming, and good-natured person.

On the other hand, you have probably also been in situations where you felt as if you did everything wrong and thus probably led others to think you were a clod. Why did this happen? You might say, "I had a bad day." That might be true, but if we are sociologically mindful, we will see that there is more to it, that having a good day or a bad day has a lot to do with what happens between people. Others can bring out the best or the worst in us.

If others show interest in what we say, if they respect our opinions, if they laugh at our jokes, then we will probably perform better—that is, speak more smoothly and confidently, with more wit and charm— than if they look away when we speak, remain silent at our jokes, or dismiss our opinions. By affecting our performances, others thus help make us who we are in a situation. If their behavior elicits a fine performance on our part, they will have evidence from which to infer that we have good qualities. If they treat us in a way that makes us foul up, then they will have a bad performance from which to infer that we are inept.

Again, it goes both ways; we affect others' performances, too. This is not just a matter of treating others in ways that let them show the best of who they are. Sometimes it is a matter of accepting others' claims to being a little better than they are. A friend might boast a bit, exaggerating some quality or feat. Do we let the boast pass without comment, or do we challenge it? Whichever we do, our action will affect the image the friend is trying to create. Others can likewise support or challenge the claims we make about ourselves.

These images upon which others rely to make inferences about our character are thus social creations. We can't make images by ourselves. And the exact images—and therefore the "virtual selves" that others impute to us—depend on what we can pull off with various audiences. But there are even more profound ways in which this creation of images and virtual selves depends on social life.

Resources for Creating Images

Consider what it takes to create a favorable image of one's self. We must be able to present the signs—in the forms of speech, behavior, and material objects (e.g., clothing)—that others can use to make inferences about us. All these resources come from social life. We must learn how to speak and act in ways that others will interpret as signs of competence, morality, or other good qualities. We must also acquire certain resources (skills, money) that will allow us to obtain other signifying resources, such as a good job, nice clothes, a car and a home, and so on. In other words, all the signs that we can muster to create images, impressions, and creditable selves are products of social life, as is the ability to use these signs in an impressive way.

Perhaps you are thinking, "Sure, signs come from social life, and so does the ability to use them. So what?" The answer is this: In a society where there is a great deal of inequality, the resources and skills necessary to signify a creditable self will be unequally distributed. This means that not everyone can create a creditable self, at least with some audiences. It also means that some people will be able to create impressions of goodness by virtue of their power, rather than by the power of their virtue.

Being sociologically mindful, we will pay attention to who is able to access and wield what kinds of signs, who learns how to use them properly, and who gets a chance to use them with certain audiences. We will also ask, "Who gets to say what will be taken as an important sign of character?" This is part of being mindful about why, in U.S. society, a male body, light skin, Caucasian features, an Anglo-Saxon surname, heterosexual inclinations, and wealth are interpreted as signs of a worthy self.

We should try to be mindful, then, that images matter because they affect how we treat others and how they treat us; that images are not the result of personalities but of how people define things, how people treat each other, and how much inequality exists between groups in a society; and that people in dominant groups can use their advantages to create images of their own competence and morality, while denying people in less powerful groups the resources to create images of equal value. Part of being sociologically mindful is paying attention to how such images are created, how they affect people's chances for good lives, and how they help to maintain (or to change) the way the social world works.

Representations

A student once told me that "The Sixties" was a time of rampant drug use, wild sex, permissiveness, anti-Americanism, and widespread social disorder. His point was that nothing good had come out of the 1960s, and that it was best to put that foolish and destructive era behind us. I asked him when he was born. "Nineteen-seventy-five," he said. How could he know so much about the 1960s? "Various sources," he said. When I pressed him to be more specific, he admitted that he had not read any books about the 1960s but had gained his knowledge "from TV and stuff."

There is nothing wrong with learning about distant times, places, and people from television, but we should be mindful that television offers us knowledge in the form of representations that are usually designed more to entertain than to inform. This means that someone, or some group of people, has selected for us a part of the picture— a subset of all that could be known about something else—and presented it to us as if it were the whole picture. What we thus get is a crafted, partial re-presentation of a reality to which we might have no direct access.

The student who told me about the 1960s had not checked out the representations he had been given. If he had, he might have learned that during the 1960s, most college students did not protest or riot, take drugs, or participate in orgies, and while many repressive aspects of U.S. society—racism, sexism, imperialism, militarism—were challenged through polite and impolite protest, there was mostly business as usual, not "widespread social disorder." He might also have learned that many of the gains in civil rights that he took for granted were made during the 1960s.

Of course, even if this student read books about the 1960s and talked to people who lived through that time, he would still be relying on representations. Not having been there, and having no way to go back and see for himself, he had no choice but to rely on representations created by others. Unfortunately, the student relied on representations that were clichés or stereotypes and did not question how or why they were created.

When an *image* is being created, the creator of the image—or the thing for which an image is being created—is there for us to see. A *representation* is an image of a distant reality: times, places, people, things, and events to which we do not have immediate or direct access. To talk about what the 1960s were like, or what the Chinese are like, or what the dark side of the moon is like, or what a quark is like, or what happened last week at a party, is to create a representation. The representation brings the distant reality into the here and now.

The Necessity and Danger of Representations

Like images, representations are indispensable. If we are going to talk about distant realities at all, we must create representations of them. Also like images, representations are created with help or hindrance from others. Sometimes others affirm our representations ("Yeah, that's how it happened"); sometimes they offer competing versions of their own ("Let me tell you what *really* happened!"), in which case we might have to do some revising. The representations we finally agree upon are usually the result of negotiation.

Being sociologically mindful, we see not only that representations are indispensable, but that what we take reality to be depends on the particular representations we create and agree upon. Failing to be mindful, we may fail to see that representations are indeed re-presentations and we may mistake them for an unmediated view of reality. If we are not mindful of representations as re-presentations, we may also fail to see how they are often distorted to serve the interests of their creators.

A student once told me about a TV program that purported to show real cops in action. I said that he should not take the program too seriously because its representations of police work were probably fabricated to make them more entertaining. The student insisted that the program showed events exactly as they happened. I could not convince him otherwise until I found an article, written by a person who had helped produce the program, explaining how the apparently real crime scenes were contrived. The student then realized that he had been fooled, but no doubt millions of people believed that the program was an unfiltered, accurate portrayal of distant realities.

Being sociologically mindful, we should be suspicious of representations—like the cop show—that claim *not* to be constructed. We should be suspicious because someone is trying to convince us what a distant reality is like while hiding the fact that they are choosing how to represent that reality to us. If we are mindful, we will always see representations as constructed, and then we'll ask who is doing the constructing, how, for whom, and why. Sometimes the answers will be obvious, sometimes not. In any case, if we ask the questions, we are less likely to be taken in.

It is important to be wary of representations precisely because we are so dependent upon them. Consider all the matters that are represented to us: historical events and eras; events in other countries; the state of our own economy; the character of the leaders and people in other countries; the actions of corporations and of governments; the various worlds of scientific research. In some cases, we may have direct access to what is being represented. When we don't, which is most of the time, we would be wise to examine representations from several sources and, again, to consider how they are constructed, with what interests in mind.

Misrepresentation by Stereotype and Habit

To be sociologically mindful of how representations are constructed does not mean presuming that all representations are designed to fool us. Some *are* designed to fool us, of course. If a mining corporation, for example, is represented (by its public-relations firm) as a champion of environmental preservation, the fakery is easy to see. But it can also happen that misleading representations are created as a matter of cultural habit, by people with no intent to deceive.

Suppose you heard a 30-second news story (a typical length for radio or television) about a 6-year-old boy who was charged by school administrators with sexual harassment for kissing a classmate on the cheek. You might think, "This has gone too far! A legitimate concern about sexual harassment has turned into hysteria. It's crazy to charge a six-year-old with sexual harassment!" Your reaction would be understandable. Many people would react the same way. But here is another possible reaction: "Could there be more to the story?"

It might turn out that knowing more of the story would make a difference. Suppose you knew that the boy had been bothering several of his classmates for a long time; that the boy had resisted gentler efforts to discipline him; that the school administrators had been sued previously for failing to take action against a slightly older boy who engaged in the same kind of misbehavior; and that the administrators were reluctant to invoke the sexual harassment charge but felt they had no choice, since the boy's parents refused to cooperate in disciplining him. If you knew all this, you might feel differently about the situation.

The point of this example is not just that more information can lead to a more intelligent response to a situation, but that complex situations are often represented in stereotypical ways. In this example, a story that was too complex to fit into 30 seconds was reduced to a cliché: "Overzealous administrators go to absurd lengths to be politically correct." This sort of reporting is common, though not because of a conspiracy to deny the seriousness of sexual harassment. It happens because stereotypes are helpful for quickly creating easy-to-grasp representations of complex distant realities.

Much the same kind of stereotyping had affected my student's view of "The Sixties." He had no doubt been exposed to many representations of the 1960s as a time of irresponsible youthful rebellion. This stereotypical representation, because it was so frequently used, came to seem like the version of reality upon which everyone agreed. Not knowing any better, and having no good reason to be suspicious, he accepted it.

All representations are incomplete and simplified. There is no avoiding that. What we can avoid, if we are sociologically mindful, is being caught in the illusion that representations are direct views to distant realities. What we see, in other words, is the *constructedness* of representations. Again, this does not mean dismissing all representations as fantasies contrived to mislead us. It means paying attention to how representations are constructed, by whom, to serve what purposes.

In some cases it might be clear why some person or group would like us to accept a particular representation. We might see, for example, that if we accept one group's representation of history, then this will make them seem like victims of injustice who are deserving of our sympathy and support. To recognize that people have an interest in portraying history in a particular way does not make their representation of history correct or incorrect; it simply alerts us to look for bias and to seek more information.

Perhaps most simply, to be sociologically mindful about representations is to ask, What else is there to know about these people or events? How is the version I am being offered shaped, consciously or unconsciously, by the values and interests of its source? Has this representation been constructed through careful investigation, or is it just hearsay? Who might represent things differently? Why? If such questions habitually come to mind, we are less likely to be taken in by stereotypes or duped by malicious fabricators.

Giving and Receiving Accounts

Suppose that you are going to miss a deadline. To avoid being penalized, you can ask for an extension. To get the extension, you must give an acceptable account for why your work is late. For example, you might say, "My work is late because I am lazy, irresponsible, and don't care if my behavior hurts anyone else. But if you'll give me an extension, I'll get the work done when I feel like it." That is one possible account. The person who hears it might at least give you credit for honesty.

Here is another possible account: "I'm sorry my work is late. I really tried to get it done, but my father got laid off this week, and my mother got sick right after she came home from my aunt's funeral, and I've had to put in extra hours at the store because of the holiday season. So things are a real mess right now, and I got a little behind. But if you could give me some extra time, I think I can get the work done in a day or so." Unless the person who hears this is coldhearted, or thinks you are a baldfaced liar, you will probably get the extension.

As long as we do what others expect us to, we do not usually have to give accounts. It is only when our behavior is unexpected, or violates a rule, that we have to account for it, perhaps with a justification or an excuse. Like images, accounts matter. The right account can make the difference between getting an extension on a deadline or getting fired, between being acquitted or being found guilty, between saving a relationship or losing it. To keep social life working smoothly, and to avoid trouble for ourselves, we must know how to give proper accounts.

Perhaps you are thinking, "This giving of accounts wouldn't be such a big deal if people just told the truth all the time. The truth is always the best account." That is a noble sentiment, perhaps, but in real life things are more complicated, since the truth can be told more or less completely, and in different ways.

Suppose that a friend tells you about a problem s/he is having, in hopes that you will listen and show understanding. Instead, you brush off the problem as trivial and thus hurt your friend's feelings. Perhaps later s/he calls you to account for your behavior. What can you say? The truth might be that you like this friend very much but are tired of all the obsessing about problems that seem small to you. So you might say, "I wasn't listening closely because I was tired of your whining about penny-ante troubles while there are people starving in the world." That account might end the friendship. If you didn't want that to happen, you could try this: "I do care about how you feel. It's just hard for me sometimes to understand why certain things affect you so strongly. And when I don't understand why you feel the way you do, I get impatient and drift off while you're talking. I'm sorry."

As this example suggests, it is not the truth that determines how an audience will react to an account. What matters is the account itself—how it is shaped, the reality it implies, and the feelings it evokes. As with images, there is no way around this reliance on accounts, since the truth, whatever it might be and no matter how much we might want to tell it, is tellable only through accounts. There is no getting at it directly.

If you showed up at work wearing only a robe made from pages out of this book, you would surely be called to account for your attire. If you said, "I am dressed like this because it's a hot day and this is a cool book," you would probably be seen as crazy, sent home, or fired. Some accounts just don't fly, and again, it's not truth that makes the difference. An account works when it is plausible and reasonable to the audience hearing it. Members of a fan club might think it perfectly fine to wear pages from a book written by the club's hero.

Behind and Underneath Accounts

If we pay attention to how accounts are fashioned, we can see what it is that people take for granted. For example, if you ask someone, "Why did you get so drunk last night?" and that person says, "Because I lost my job and was feeling awful," you might be inclined to accept this account. You might say, "I understand." Now consider what is taken for granted here: Jobs are important, losing a job is a big deal, bad feelings should be escaped, and drinking is an effective way to escape them. If you did not take these matters for granted, the other person's account for getting drunk would make no sense.

Accounts work because the givers and receivers of accounts share certain assumptions. Every account, if viewed mindfully, can thus be a way to see deeper into the shared beliefs that hold a community together. To see these beliefs we must ask, "Why does this account work? What assumptions must be accepted for this account to seem plausible and reasonable?" To practice this kind of mindfulness we do not have to go looking for accounts to study. We can begin by paying more attention to our own.

There might be many people—teachers, bosses, politicians, corporate executives, administrators, bureaucrats—from whom you would like to demand accounts. Perhaps you think that some such people should be forced to explain what they are doing and why. And if they can't give acceptable accounts, then they should be fired, defrocked, booted out of office, put in jail, or punished in some other way. The problem, however, is that your demands for accounts (you could write angry letters to the editor of the local paper) would probably be ignored. Who are you, after all, to demand an account from Chancellor Phogmann, Senator Lootscam, or the president of BioDynaTek?

Obviously, there is a connection between power and accountability. In fact, a good index of a person's power is how free that person is to ignore others' demands for accounts. Having power also means being able to force others to account for their actions, under threat of punishment if they don't comply. Being mindful of who feels obligated to give accounts to whom, of who can force others to give accounts, and of who can ignore demands for giving accounts, is thus a way to see the inequality that exists in a group, organization, community, or nation.

Tools for Making Reality

Being sociologically mindful, we can see that social reality is constructed in part by formulating and giving accounts. In giving accounts, people say what they think is real—or what they want others to believe is real. And when accounts are accepted, it is as if an agreement has been made: "Okay, I/we accept this account as a description of what is the case; we will proceed from here." Perhaps, then, you can see why it is important to be mindful of how accounts are formulated, given, and judged. It is because in this process a social reality is being created that we may all be stuck with for a while.

Perhaps it seems that images and accounts are one thing and reality is another. There is a sense in which this is true. An image can be false, in that it can be crafted to produce incorrect inferences about the character of a person or a group. An account can be false, too, in the sense that it does not faithfully correspond to how things actually are or were—as might be found out through an impartial and careful investigation. On the other hand, we have no choice but to rely on images and accounts in determining what is real. A false image can be replaced only by another image, just as a false account can be challenged only by another account.

Being sociologically mindful, we see that there is no getting around our reliance on images, representations, and accounts, for it is only by fashioning images, representations, and accounts that we can create shared beliefs about what is real and true. We see, in other words, that our ideas about what is real and true depend on a process from which we cannot escape—a process of creating and acting on appearances. With this awareness, we can then become better analysts of who creates what kinds of appearances, for what purposes, and with what results for whom.

Significant Absences

Suppose you have just met a person whom you find attractive and would like to impress. You've heard that this person values honesty, so when this person asks, "What do you do?" instead of talking about your job you say, "I pick my nose when no one is looking. I clip my toenails in the sink. I toss dirty socks on the floor around my hamper. And sometimes I go for months without changing the sheets on my bed." In this case, your honesty will probably backfire. The other person might say, "Hmmm, well, yes, that's interesting. I'd like to talk more, but right now I have to rotate my tires. Good-bye."

What did you do wrong? You were just trying to craft an image of yourself as an honest person in the eyes of someone you thought would appreciate it. And it's not as if you admitted to being a serial killer or a tobacco company executive. So what was the problem?

This silly example makes two serious points. One is that violating cultural rules about what is appropriate to tell about yourself, on what occasions, can lead others to see you as inept. To put it another way, following the usual rules about how to present ourselves to others is part of crafting an image of ourselves as sane, normal, and safe to be around. A second point is that appearances are crafted by leaving certain things out of the picture. When crafting images of ourselves, we must know what to tell and what not to tell, or else we are likely to spoil the image.

You have no doubt learned that when meeting others it is usually best to lead off with positive information about yourself, so as to make a good first impression. Then, once you have convinced others that you are a decent person, you can gradually reveal your flaws. If you put all the bad news up front, you will probably have a hard time salvaging a creditable image of yourself later. To create a good impression, you must know what to leave out.

The absence of information is important when it comes to creating representations. For example, the history of the United States can be represented like this: "Once upon a time, brave European explorers discovered a vast, untamed land, which was later settled by colonists seeking freedom from rule by kings and popes. Eventually these colonists fought a war to break their ties to a corrupt English king. After thus freeing themselves, the colonists built a new republic, founded on principles of liberty and democracy. The republic grew and, over the next 200 years, expanded to reach the far sea, turning an undeveloped land into the richest, most productive, freest nation on earth."

That is an impressive, even inspiring, representation, much like what is taught in grade-school civics courses. It is, however, a representation that achieves a positive effect by leaving out important things. Specifically, it does not mention that the "vast, untamed land" was already populated by indigenous peoples, most of whom were killed to make way for European settlers; it does not mention the enslavement of Africans or the fact that "liberty and democracy" were originally intended only for white men who owned land; and it does not mention the expansion of the United States by the violent theft of land from Mexico. To put these matters back in the picture makes for quite a different representation.

Organized Exclusion and Invention

Representations of groups of people are also shaped by absences. For example, if books or films that tell about great scientists, philosophers, writers, and politicians never mention Africans or women, it will thus appear that women and Africans are not capable of achievement in these fields. A careful study of U.S. history shows, however, that Africans and women have done outstanding work as scientists, philosophers, writers, politicians, and so on. But if their work is overlooked in official accounts of who has done great things, then an unjust, inaccurate, and harmful representation is created. In this way, representations of groups—like images of selves and repre-sentations of nations—are created by leaving things out of the picture.

Perhaps you have noticed that there is a difference between how images of selves are created in everyday life and how representations of nations and groups are created. When you create an image of yourself, you do so in collaboration with a small group of others, usually in face-to-face interaction. Even if people affect your image by talking behind your back, it is still likely to be done informally, by a small number of people. Rarely in everyday life is there an organized effort, involving more than a few people, to destroy or uphold the image of an individual person.

In contrast, creating representations of types of people and of nations requires cooperation on a large scale. For example, it requires the cooperation of many people—writers, publishers, teachers, school boards, and parents—to create and uphold the sanitized representation of the United States described earlier. It also takes cooperation on a large scale to create representations of black males as violent and criminal; of feminists as angry man-haters; of working-class men as rednecks; of women as better suited to nurturing than to governing; of political leaders as competent; and so on. Representations like these—ones that come to us through television, films, newspapers, books, churches, and schools—are institutional products.

Being mindful of representations as institutional products suggests that we need to know who controls institutions and who benefits from the representations they create. This is not to say that we will always find a top boss or committee telling others to distort reality. More likely we will find a group of people who are comforted by, or derive other benefits from, creating particular representations of history, politics, other people, and so on. We might also find that many people who take part in creating representations act on habit and do not think to question the assumptions underlying their work.

Seeing how representations are created institutionally can also help us understand why some representations are so widespread and hard to change. It is not because people stupidly insist on believing what is false, but because they are constantly fed misleading representations that are passed off as true. If these representations come from institutional sources—the mass media, schools, government— they can be hard to escape and hard to refute; they also seem to have a great deal of authority. If a teacher says, "You must read this book to learn," we are more likely to fear being bored than being misled.

Challenging Representations

To change well-established, institutionally created representations requires an organized effort. Rarely is it enough to speak out alone and say, "That is untrue! Here is how things really are. . . ." Of course, speaking what we see as the truth is worth doing because even if it turns out that we are wrong, more will be learned if we speak up than if we don't. But if we are convinced that an institutionally created representation is wrong, then we must work with others to change it, perhaps by creating a newspaper, a school, an anti-defamation league, or a think tank. The absence of challenge, like the absence of information, is part of what allows false representations to stand.

Being sociologically mindful about images, accounts, and representations means seeing them as constructed. It also means suspecting, as a matter of habit, that something has been left out, that what we are seeing contains significant absences. If we are offered no view of the dark side of what is represented to us, we should suspect that such a side exists and keep an eye open for it. The purpose of such wariness is not to debunk everything that seems too good to be true, but to be able to see all things more fully and honestly, and as more complex than first appearances might suggest.

If we are sociologically mindful, we will look for alternative images, accounts, and representations and try to create our own picture of things—of people, places, events, history, groups, and so on—rather than accepting the pictures that are handed to us. Only by doing this can we find out if there are alternative versions of reality, and if other versions have been suppressed. Being mindful in this way, we may also discover the significant absences in official accounts of reality. We will see, too, how appearances are linked to power. At the same time, by being sociologically mindful of how appearances are constructed, by and for whom, we will develop our own power to see more deeply into how the social world works.

RELATED READINGS

Brissett, Dennis, & Edgley, Charles. (1990). *Life As Theater* (2nd ed.). New York: Aldine.

Farr, Robert M., & Moscovici, Serge. (1984). *Social Representations*. London: Cambridge University Press.

Goffman, Erving. (1959). *The Presentation of Self in Everyday Life*. Garden City, NY: Doubleday.

Herman, Edward, & Chomsky, Noam. (1988). *Manufacturing Consent: The Political Economy of the Mass Media*. New York: Pantheon.

Parenti, Michael. (1986). *Inventing Reality*. New York: St. Martin's.

Scott, Marvin, & Lyman, Stanford. (1968). "Accounts." *American Sociological Review* 33:46–62.

CHAPTER TEN

Understanding Power in Social Life

One time I told my class about an angry professor who wanted to take over the university. His plan was to march into the chancellor's office, tell him to pack up and move along, and declare himself in charge. My students laughed. I said, "Is this funny? Don't you think his plan would work?" No one thought it would work. Most thought the professor would end up in jail or in a psychiatric hospital. I said that that wasn't necessarily true.

"What if the professor *explains* to the chancellor why it would be wise for him to step aside? Wouldn't that make for a smooth transition?" I asked. One student said that this wouldn't work, either, because the chancellor would call the campus cops to haul the professor away. I said that the professor could just explain to the cops why they ought to support him and not the old chancellor.

Another student said it still wouldn't work. She said that even if the professor convinced every cop on campus to accept him as the new chancellor, no one else would. "Who else matters?" I asked. "If the cops support the professor, isn't that enough?" One student said that to be accepted as chancellor, the professor would need the support of state legislators, the governor, other professors, and staff. She also said that if he didn't follow the proper procedure for getting the chancellor's job, he'd never get the support of these people.

I said that the professor just needed to write a pamphlet explaining how the old chancellor had botched the job and should be replaced. Then if everyone read the pamphlet, they would understand why it was time for change and why they should support the professor when he took over. Some students shook their heads; some squirmed in their chairs. I heard at least one sigh. There was a lot of doubt in the room.

The student who was fond of procedure said, "This whole thing is crazy. If people could take over by doing what you're talking about doing, there would be chaos. There would be no legitimate authority, and there'd be constant fighting." Another student said, "The plan isn't crazy at all—but it is scary, because it could work. I mean, how does anyone get legitimate authority in the first place? It probably always comes out of a fight."

I said that "legitimate authority" could be created in various ways, but that *power* on a large scale always depends on shared belief and people working together. Neither presidents nor revolutionaries have power in a vacuum; they always need the support of others, if only a few disciples at first. What's more, getting the support of others requires resources created by a human community: language, ideas, money, media, weapons, and food. Being sociologically mindful, we can see, then, that power arises out of social life, not out of charismatic personalities.

It isn't necessary to be a boss in an organization to have power. To be able to make something happen somewhere is to have power, no matter how little it might be. Still, this power depends on social life, since this is where our skills, knowledge, motivation, and even bodies come from. Even though we don't need to be bosses to make things happen, we still ultimately depend on others for whatever power we have.

Ideas and Illusions

An old saying has it that "power comes from the barrel of a gun." This is true in the sense that guns can be used to coerce people, since most people would rather obey just about any order than be shot. And when groups are fighting, the side with the most guns usually wins. So guns can indeed be used to make things happen. Here is another old saying: "Give me a child for the first five years, and s/he will be mine for life." This second saying contradicts the first because it says that what a person can be made to do depends on what s/he is taught. So which is more powerful, ideas or guns?

Suppose you had lots of guns and you got an itch to overthrow a government. Do you have enough guns to do the job? No number is enough unless you can find people willing to use them. Unless you can convince followers to use the guns to shoot other people, your revolution will go no further. You might as well sell your guns for scrap.

Suppose you are the ruler of Upper Slobovia. Suppose that your awful policies have sparked a movement to oust you from office. One day 50,000 people march on the capital, so you call in the police, the army, and the palace guard to protect you. As the protesters storm the palace, you give the order to shoot to kill. What happens? Nothing, because the police, soldiers, and guards think the protesters are right and you are corrupt. The protesters succeed because their ideas have made your guns useless.

Power is plain to see when guns are used to coerce people. It is not so easy to see, however, when ideas are used to shape people's thoughts and desires. If a rebel leader says, "Let me tell you why the government is corrupt and why the Shining Militia should be in charge," that is an obvious attempt to use ideas to gain power. A direct approach like this would of course put you on guard, lest you be persuaded to support an outrageous movement. Suppose, however, that ideas are used more subtly, and used on those least able to defend themselves.

Think of children in schools. If you were the leader of a country (or a member of a group that benefited from what the leaders were doing), and you wanted to preserve the social arrangements you had created, you might develop a plan like this:

- Every morning in every class in every school, students will face the flag, join hands, and recite the Pledge of Unity, collectively raising their hands over their heads when they come to the lines "My heart for my land/When I hear my land's call/God's blessings will be upon us/My country above all."

- Students at the elementary level will be required to study the history of our nation, from the time when the first settlers began pushing back the savage frontier up to the present. The objective will be to help students appreciate the great progress in civilization that has resulted from the heroic efforts of our nation's founders and later leaders.

- Students at the secondary level will be required to take at least one course in comparative government. The objective will be to help students see that our system of government offers the best possible balance between freedom and equality. Other systems will be examined to see how they fall short of this ideal.

- Students at the secondary level will be required to take at least one course in comparative economy. The objective will be to help students see that our economic system provides everyone with an equal chance to succeed, and that differences in wealth result from natural differences in talent.

■ While schools will not be required to comply with this plan, special funds will be available to schools and school districts that do. Funds can be used for construction, teacher salaries, travel, equipment, and hiring of staff. Funds will be distributed in the form of block grants to approved schools and districts, with expenditures controlled by local administrators.

This is just one way you could try to instill ideas that will encourage people to accept things as they are, including the fact that you are in charge. If you can instill these ideas in school, when people are very young, they may never think of thinking differently. This is a more efficient and durable way to control people than holding guns on them.

Instilling Needs

Another possibility (and for this you don't need to control a government) is to use ideas to instill needs in people—needs that only you, or your product, can satisfy. If you can create a situation like this, people will want to give you things—money, adoration, or obedience—so as to get from you what they desire. Here is an example of how this could happen.

Imagine you are the chief executive officer of BioDynaTek. Profits are falling, and you need to revive them by increasing sales. So you've told your research lab to come up with a hot new product. After several years of work, one of the lab teams invents a way to build eyeglasses that look ordinary but can project a small computer-like screen, visible only to the wearer, on which can be displayed information from memory chips hidden in the earpieces. Users of the glasses can thus have all kinds of information available at the tips of their eyeballs.

Your engineers and accountants calculate that your Virtual Memory Vision™ glasses can be sold at about the same price as a cellular phone—not cheap but still affordable for a lot of middle-class folks. Your marketing people think that VMV glasses could sell big and revive BioDynaTek's sagging profits, so you decide to manufacture and sell the glasses yourself for a few years to establish the market, and then license the technology to other companies.

There is, however, one problem: No one feels a need for VMV glasses. What you must do, therefore, is create a need for your product. Your advertising people are paid to do exactly this sort of thing. So you turn the problem over to them, and soon they come up with several ways to pitch VMV glasses. They suggest television ads like these:

- A man arrives home after a day at the office. Child or partner sees he is empty-handed and says, "You forgot, *again?*" Cut to man leaving work and checking VMV calendar display; man sees reminder to buy birthday gift; man arrives home and delivers gift to delighted partner or child. Message: VMV glasses can prevent the embarrassment and hurt feelings that come from forgetting important dates, such as birthdays and anniversaries. Catch phrase: "VMV. Because love means never having to say 'I forgot.'"

- A professional type (physician, lawyer, stockbroker) is asked a question in a tense meeting and fumbles for an answer. Cut to irritated/anxious look on face of boss/client. Second professional type—wearing VMV glasses—speaks up and crisply delivers the right answer. Cut to approving nod and smile from boss/client. Message: VMV glasses are the solution to the otherwise impossible task of keeping up with current knowledge in any business or professional field. Catch phrase: "VMV. When it's important to know. Now."

- A couple stands on a busy big-city street corner, apparently looking for something. One leafs through a tattered address book and says, "I thought it was right here, but I guess we missed it. We'd better head back." The other, wearing VMV glasses (and more fashionably dressed), tilts head down and says, "Hold on, let me check. I see. It's just moved around the block. C'mon, we've got plenty of time." Message: Smart, successful, sophisticated people use VMV glasses to manage modern life and still have time for fun. Catch phrase: "VMV. For people who refuse to let life get away from them."

These ads don't try to argue people into buying your product. Instead they arouse people's insecurities about appearing insensitive, incompetent, or uncool—and then suggest that these insecurities can be relieved by a product they had never heard of before. If these ads work, BioDynaTek will make millions from the sale of VMV glasses.

The point here is not about how to sell high-tech hokum, but about how ideas can be used to get others to do what you want. One way is to get others to feel a need for what you have to give. Even more power can come from getting people to think that only you can give them what they want. Instilling such ideas makes others dependent on you, in which case you can demand from them what you want. If the need is strong enough, people will meet very high demands.

Using ideas to instill feelings of need and dependency is not just an advertising ploy. It is quite common and does not require the resources of a corporation. Being sociologically mindful, we can see that power is created in this way in many places. We can also see that there is great potential for harm in this way of creating power.

For example, suppose that one person in a relationship feels insecure about his or her looks or intelligence. If the other person wants to control the relationship, s/he can exploit this insecurity by saying, "Yes, you are flawed—so badly that no one else would want you. I, however, am willing to overlook your problems and be with you anyway. For this you should feel lucky and grateful, and be willing to meet my needs, or else I will dump you and leave you to the miserable fate you deserve." Such messages are usually conveyed more subtly. The effect is to make a person feel dependent, which is likely to make the person more controllable.

Sometimes this happens between teachers and students. Perhaps a teacher feels threatened by a student's growing knowledge and confidence. To put the student back in place, the teacher might say, "You think you're so smart? Ha! Compared to me you are still an ignoramus. And remember, I'll be writing your letters of recommen-dation, so don't get uppity." The teacher is trying to reassert control by reminding the student that s/he still depends on the teacher for many things. It is this dependence, plus the student's desire for what the teacher can give, that cements the teacher's power over the student.

Impeding Critical Thought

Other ideas help to sustain power by making change seem impossible or foolish. For example, while it is easy to show that an economy driven by greed is harmful to humans and to the earth, when this point is made in regard to capitalism, many people will say, "Capitalism may not be perfect, but the only alternative is communism, which no one wants because it would take away all our property and freedoms." I have heard this often in the classroom.

What many people seem to believe is that there is no good alternative to capitalism, and that much of what we enjoy about life in our society would be lost if major change were attempted. These ideas make it hard to think seriously about what could be done to make better lives possible for more people. By impeding critical thought and conversation, these ideas help to maintain the current system and the privileges of those who enjoy power within it.

The idea that if things change they will only get worse is much older than capitalism. Whenever people have tried to hold onto power the same idea has cropped up. The ideas that current arrangements, whatever they might be, are the best possible and that everything good in life depends on sticking to these arrangements are used to make people fear change and feel that it is wise and mature to accept society as it is.

But people are not always so easily discouraged. In many instances people have felt that some arrangement was too unjust or painful to bear, so they began to struggle for change. The civil rights and women's movements in the United States are two examples; the overthrow of the apartheid regime in South Africa is another. We could make a long list of similar examples. In each case we would find people who refused to accept the idea that change was impossible or foolish.

The powerful do often succeed, however, in using ideas to hold onto power. Perhaps it will help to show how else this might be done. Many of the ideas used to hold onto power are well-worn by now, though they are still effective if an audience does not think critically. The leaders of a government that is being challenged by revolutionaries might use any or all of the following ideas to defend themselves:

- You who are threatening our great society are engaged in a futile effort. You do not have the resources, the leadership, the vision, or the popular support to win control. Our forces are superior in every way. What's more, God is on our side and he has told us not to relinquish our responsibilities to govern. So it is clear that you cannot prevail. It would be best now if you ceased your wasteful struggle and returned quietly to your everyday lives.

■ You who are demanding change are reckless and foolish. You are not competent to run this complex society of ours. In fact, you should be grateful that we who are of superior spirit and intellect are willing to do it. If you think there is something wrong with how things are being done, let us know, and we will look into your complaints. If we determine that they are valid, we will take appropriate action. You must trust us to look after the best interests of all.

■ You who are causing disruption are being misled. Your leaders do not really care about your needs or well-being. They simply want you to take risks for their benefit. If you follow them, they will sacrifice you to satisfy their own lust for power. Our purpose, unlike theirs, is to serve you by keeping our society operating peacefully and productively. So please turn away from your corrupt leaders before it is too late. Let us all try to feel like good neighbors again.

As you can see, political speechwriters and advertising copywriters have much in common. When they are paid to do it, both know how to use ideas to generate doubt, undermine feelings of strength and hope, and cloud people's thinking. They have mastered the art of using ideas as resources to make things happen or to keep them from happening.

Because this sort of manipulation is so common, you might think, "I won't believe any of the crap I'm told. It's all lies. I will doubt *everything*." This is a posture of radical skepticism, and I suppose it is better, or less dangerous, than believing everything you are told. It is impossible, however, to doubt everything. We always have to make sense of the world from some point of view, and this means taking certain ideas for granted (if we really doubted everything, we couldn't function at all). Rather than trying to doubt everything, it is perhaps better to be skeptical in a disciplined way.

It is clear that ideas are often used to create, acquire, and hold onto power, and we should be wary of this. Being sociologically mindful can help, because we will think to ask, Where did this idea come from? Who would like me to believe it? Who will benefit and who will be hurt if a lot of people believe it and act on it? Remembering to ask these questions makes us less vulnerable to manipulation. Of course, sociological mindfulness does not ensure that we will find true answers. It is merely a way of seeing that makes us less likely to be taken in by what is false and harmful.

Controlling Information

If I asked how many candidates ran for president in the last U.S. presidential election, would you say "two"? That is the usual answer. Some people will vaguely recall a third-party candidate and say "three." Others will think of the primaries, add those candidates, and guess "eight or ten." The correct answer is "over 200."

Most people are surprised to learn this. Perhaps you think, "Yes, that is more than I expected, but those aren't all serious candidates. A lot of them probably file the papers and pay the fee just to say that they 'ran for president.'" You would be right; for many of the 200, running for president is a lark. Yet many more than two candidates can offer intelligent policy statements. Usually about 30 candidates are at least this serious.

Perhaps one or more of these alternative candidates has ideas and plans that would appeal to you. Unfortunately, you will probably never know if this is the case, because information about these people and their ideas is filtered out by the very organizations that are supposed to bring it to you. If we consider how and why this happens, we can gain some understanding of how power often rests on the control of information.

One reason that alternative candidates are ignored is that media people see them as having no chance to win. Media people are right. Restrictive election rules and the high cost of television advertising make it hard for alternative candidates to compete. But what truly dooms them is a lack of coverage. In this way, a self-fulfilling prophecy is created. Alternative candidates are not covered because they are seen as having no chance to win, and they have no chance to win if they are not covered.

Some candidates' ideas also get filtered out because they are considered unrealistic. For example, a candidate who wanted to cut military spending by three-fourths and use the money to build schools, mass transit, and affordable housing, and to provide free education and medical care to everyone, would not be taken seriously by the media. Why? Because corporations and the very rich would resist such changes so fiercely that any candidate who proposed them would find it nearly impossible to win. Journalists who covered a candidate who held ideas like these would be accused of wasting time on a crank.

Perhaps you can see the problem here. If the media will cover only "serious candidates," and only those candidates whose policies do not threaten corporate power are considered serious, then voters will not hear the ideas of candidates who propose more fundamental changes in how the economy works. That information is filtered out. Alternative candidates can *say* what they want, but without coverage, few people will hear. To most voters it thus seems like everybody pretty much agrees that nothing basic needs changing and that no one has any good ideas about how to change things anyway.

People-Filtering and Self-Censorship

You might think, "Ah, he has exposed a dastardly conspiracy! No doubt the media bosses meet with the bosses of other corporations to plan all this out. To protect their own capitalist backsides, the media bosses agree to ignore radical candidates and to fire any reporters who show anti-corporate sympathies. No wonder it is so hard to change things or even to get new ideas into the system." Actually, that is not what I am saying. Being sociologically mindful, we can see why such a crude conspiracy is unnecessary.

We should see, first of all, that people who work for media corporations—as janitors, secretaries, reporters, editors, producers, or executives—are products of a culture in which capitalism and extreme inequality are taken for granted. And so it takes no special coercion to get media people to accept capitalism as normal. In fact, that's how they're likely to think when they show up looking for work.

Media people also learn that being too critical of government or corporations will get them labeled "extreme" or, worse, "biased." It is better for their careers, reporters learn, to stay within the bounds of conventional political opinion. To give serious attention to an alternative candidate, or to make an issue of a candidate's embrace of capitalism, would be seen as strange and would probably be suicidal for a journalist's career. A boss might wonder, "Doesn't this person know what the real story is? Maybe this person is in the wrong business."

And so no conspiracy is necessary for information to get filtered in a way that favors those in power. All that is required is a little people-filtering: hiring and rewarding those who accept dominant assumptions about what is right and true, and weeding out those who think differently. The result is an organization in which everyone seems to agree about what's worth covering and what's too far out to deserve attention. Even though this is not the result of a conspiracy, we can see that it is not an accident, either. Certain resources (primarily money) are being used to create agreement about what is normal and what is far out.

All this is not to say that media people never report stories about corporate crime or political corruption. Of course they do. Such stories are usually interpreted, however, as examples of misbehavior by individuals or by individual firms. They are not seen as evidence that the system itself and the rules by which it operates are flawed. You will probably never see this kind of story on a major American television network news program: "Tonight, the first in a six-part series on what's wrong with capitalism and why socialism is the sensible alternative."

Powerful people and organizations do sometimes act in heavy-handed ways to control the flow of information to the public. News stories are sometimes squashed at high levels if they might be too damaging to political leaders or corporations. Threats of lawsuits and withdrawal of advertising dollars can also be used to influence decisions about which stories to report and how to report them. More often, however, the flow of information is controlled by self-censorship—that is, by reporters and editors doing what they know is acceptable and likely to be rewarded, and shying away from what they know will get them in trouble.

In some times and places the flow of information is controlled by coercion—"You will be shot if you print that story." But coercion takes a lot of energy and tends to breed suspicion and resistance, so it is not a smart strategy in the long run. It is more effective to control information by shaping thinking about what is good and right and true, and by offering rewards: "If you focus on what's important and interesting [in our judgment], you will get a raise and a promotion." In this way people can be conditioned to want to do what suits the interests of more powerful others.

If writers who criticize the government are killed, or if their books are burned in the streets, everyone will know that an effort is being made to control information. It is much harder to see information being controlled by shaping ideas about what can be taken for granted and about what is interesting and important. It is also hard to know when alternative points of view are being ignored or when conformist work is being rewarded inside organizations.

Information As a Resource for Power and Resistance

It is probably clear by now that acquiring and holding onto power depend in large part on the control of information. Or perhaps it is more accurate to say that power depends on shaping the content of information and controlling its flow to certain audiences. In this way consciousness can be managed so that people are usually compliant, rather than unruly.

A general principle here is that information is a resource that can be used to make things happen—which is to say that information can be a source of power. If you knew, for instance, that BioDynaTek stock was going to triple in value this year (because the company will soon announce the invention of VMV glasses), you could use that information to get rich. You could buy stock now and sell it later for a big gain.

Or suppose you knew of a job opening and knew exactly what a person should say in an interview to impress the boss and win the job. That would be valuable information to someone seeking a job. If you knew such a person, you could trade your information for a favor, or create an obligation to be repaid later. You could make some things happen and others not.

Even in intimate relationships people might seek power by controlling information. For example, if one person refuses to say how s/he feels, this keeps the other person guessing. It is as if one person is saying, "I will not tell you how I feel because then you will know what my vulnerabilities are, and perhaps you will someday use that information against me." Or it is possible that one person wants to appear emotionally tough and thus willing to walk out at any time. This too is a way to maintain power, because it can make the other person feel weak and dependent and perhaps a bit foolish for caring so much.

Being mindful of how information is linked to power, we can see that a great deal depends on context and the nature of our relationships to others. Nothing is a resource in a vacuum—not information or money or guns or anything. Power is the capacity to make things happen, but exactly what can be made to happen always depends on the context in which the resources we possess are or are not usable.

We can again use simple questions to remain mindful of how the information we receive is filtered and shaped. For instance, we can ask, What assumptions are shared by everyone whose ideas are presented on this program (or in this publication)? What issues are never discussed? What image of the government, the nation, or the economy is created by the information presented here? What would be a truly alternative, not just slightly different, point of view? Being sociologically mindful, we must *seek* answers, too, rather than letting others feed us whatever information they like.

A way to see how information is filtered and shaped—and to see what we're missing when we rely on one source—is to consult a variety of sources and to see how they compare. It also helps to remember that all stories have more than two sides. Being sociologically mindful, we will try to grasp as many sides as we can. When people are able to do this, and when they are willing to think critically, exploiters and fakers of all kinds lose their power.

Making Rules and Agendas

Tear off a corner of this page, a piece about half as big as a pencil eraser. Now pop it in your mouth and chew it up. How does it taste? Would you say it is (a) wonderful, (b) delicious, (c) delightful, (d) fantastic, or (e) superb? Perhaps you are thinking, "These are stupid choices! The paper tastes like nothing. If anything, it's kind of icky." Too bad. You must choose one of the categories above, or your choice will not be counted.

You are probably familiar with this kind of forced-choice situation. In school you were probably allowed to choose among a whole array of boring courses, and within each course you might have been allowed to choose to write a paper, do a book report, or take an exam. Or perhaps you once had a job in which you could decide whether to use a mop, a brush, or a sponge to scrub a floor.

Here is another example. Suppose you live in a country in which people choose their government representatives by voting. But suppose that it is so expensive to run for office that only those candidates whose ideas appeal to the rich can attract the money needed to mount an effective campaign. And suppose, to hark back to the earlier example, that only the candidates who can attract huge amounts of money are covered by the media. What then? The actual range of choices is likely to be very narrow. Only those candidates whose ideas and plans are acceptable to the rich and powerful will appear on the ballot. Now you are back to the choice to use a mop, a brush, or a sponge to do the same job.

Perhaps it seems as if these aren't real choices. It might seem that someone else, someone more powerful, usually decides ahead of time what we can choose from. If this is how it seems, you are probably seeing things clearly. Most of our choices are constrained in some way. Being sociologically mindful, we can see how our choices are often constrained in ways that allow others to hold onto power.

To show how this can happen, it will help to turn things upside down. Although it makes me a bit nervous to do this, I am going to turn you into a power monger for a few paragraphs. Hold still . . . — (*@*!!)—There, it's done. Now if you will please keep reading, I will later turn you back into a decent human being.

Now you are rich and powerful and want to stay that way. You could try to use the resources you control to force people to obey you, but the more force you use, the more anger and resistance you will provoke. A better strategy would be to allow people some room to make choices, because this will give them a satisfying feeling of control and will make them less angry and rebellious. The trick is to make sure that whatever people choose is acceptable to you.

How do you do this? Your best bet is to try to create rules and agendas to steer people toward doing what you want. Once these rules and agendas are accepted as legitimate, your power will be largely invisible and quite secure. At least for a time.

First of all, do *not* make a rule like this: "I will decide what the options are, and then you will pick one of these." That would not hide your power at all. People would just feel manipulated and resentful.

Here is a better rule: "A range of options consistent with organizational goals will be formulated by a committee of appointed executive officers, line managers, and staff." Rules like this are often used to control people in large organizations. What such a rule really means is this: *The bosses, who have already decided what the organization's goals are, will pick people who agree with these goals and have them come up with the same set of choices that the bosses would come up with if they were doing the job themselves.* As a smart power monger, you would know that this is a better way to get things to turn out to your liking.

Here is another case. Suppose that the ruling group to which you belong is challenged for control of the government by various small groups that want to create a more egalitarian society. Your group could use its control of the government to suppress these groups, but if you didn't want all the trouble this would cause, you could create an arrangement in which the less powerful groups felt that they had a chance to win control, when in fact this was extremely unlikely.

For example, you might devise an election system in which whoever gets over 50 percent of the votes wins and whoever gets less than 50 percent is out of luck. If you could convince people to accept this arrangement, your control of the government would be almost guaranteed, since no minority group by itself could muster enough votes for its candidate to win. Besides, your group would also have vast resources to promote its candidates. So even when you won election after election, it would look as though your success was the result of people's free choices.

Another principle to observe is that when making rules, laws, and other policies, make them appear neutral and impersonal, so that people will not blame you if they feel angry at being controlled. For you as a power monger, it is ideal if people experience the rules as "just there" to be dealt with, and not as tools that serve your interests. Then, instead of thinking about how, why, and for whom a rule has been made, people will think only of their choice to obey it or not.

Of course, ideas are still needed to make all this work. Someone must believe in the rules and be willing to enforce them for you. Once there are rules, however, it is usually easy to find enforcers, since telling others what to do is a way to have a small piece of power in a system where big power belongs to those on top. And there are always others who are eager to enforce rules because they fear that without rules the world will fall apart. It would certainly be in your interests, as the rule maker, to cultivate such fear.

Despite your best efforts as a power monger, some people still might see what's going on and say, "Wait a minute, there's no way for us to win under these rules! How can our needs be addressed and our ideas put into practice if the winner takes all and we get no representation in government? We think it's time to change to a system of proportional representation so that every group gets some sayso. That would give us something more like real democracy."

Many power mongers would react harshly to a proposal to do away with the system that ensures their power. But let us suppose that you are smart enough to know that violence breeds no end of violence and that, despite your greed and lust for power, you are not a monster. So you prefer a softer strategy.

You could try to discredit the challengers by spreading word that they are crazy, evil, or foreign spies. This might work if the challengers are few and unpopular, though such discrediting might be hard if there are others who don't like the existing system and think that the challengers have a good point. You could try to refute the challengers' claims, perhaps in a debate. But if you do this, you will give the challengers publicity and a chance to look like heroes, thus helping them attract support.

What you need is a way to neutralize the challengers' claims that the system is unfair, without arousing too much critical thinking about exactly that matter. Ideally, you would do this in a way that leaves people thinking that the system is even fairer than they imagined. So you and your staff come up with this response: "In a free society such as ours, it is important to periodically reexamine our institutions to make sure that they are working to provide fair representation for everyone. Therefore, we are forming a new twenty-member, nonpartisan study commission to review our election procedures, identify any problems, and propose ways to fine-tune our system to make it more effective for achieving our cherished democratic ideals."

Such a statement makes it seem that the system is responsive to criticism and open to change. It makes you seem like a wise and benevolent leader, eager to serve the people. These appearances will help defuse any anger stirred up by the challengers. Now go ahead and rig the game in your favor. Just load the study commission with people who think that a winner-take-all system is the best way to go. It also would be smart to appoint one person who believed in proportional representation, just to polish the impression of openness.

Most importantly, you must make sure that the commission understands its job to be fine-tuning the existing system, not over-hauling it. Thus it is crucial that the chairperson be on your side. Then if anyone proposes radical changes, the chairperson will say, "That proposal is beyond the scope of what we have been asked to do. Now, let us get down to the task at hand, as it has been given to us. We have a deadline to meet."

Power mongers must be good at setting agendas. The trick is to arrange the situation so that serious challenges to business as usual are excluded from consideration right from the start. At the same time, it is clever to allow a lot of discussion about matters that do not bring the fairness of the existing system into question. If people can be kept busy dealing with an agenda full of safe matters, they will probably not even miss what has been left off.

Autonomy and Freedom

I apologize for turning you into a power monger for these past few paragraphs. No doubt it was unpleasant for you. Just take a deep breath and sit still for a moment . . . —(!!@:))—There, I have turned you back into a decent human being.

So what does it mean to be sociologically mindful of power? It means paying attention to how resources are used, by whom, to make things happen or to keep them from happening. It means paying attention to how ideas are used, by whom, to shape thoughts and feelings and create comforting or distracting illusions. It means watching to see how information is filtered and shaped, by whom, in ways that create dependencies or keep others from acting effectively. It also means looking critically at rules and agendas to try to see who makes them, how they are made, and whose interests they serve.

Being sociologically mindful of what power is and how it works, we see it as rooted in social life—that is, in shared beliefs, in coopera-tion, and in the ways people do things together on an everyday basis. This way of seeing reminds us that power does not spring from individuals. If it did, power would be hard to resist without violence.

But since power depends on shared belief and cooperation, we can always resist power by challenging the beliefs and withholding the cooperation on which it depends. It is thus also possible to create power with others by developing new beliefs and ways of cooperating.

Being sociologically mindful, we will also be aware of the dangers that arise whenever power is created. The danger, of course, is that some people, perhaps even those who begin with the best of intentions, will be tempted to use power to make happen things that are to their advantage only. On the other hand, if many people are paying attention, and they know how to detect and resist the destructive or selfish use of power, then the danger is greatly reduced.

The point of being sociologically mindful of power is not merely to see how it works or to resist it individually. It is, rather, to see how the search for and exercise of power *over others* denies many people the freedom to create good lives. Perhaps you think, "If I can see how and when someone is trying to control me, I can evade these efforts and thus carve out a little sphere of freedom for myself." Yes, that is possible. Many people try to do exactly this.

We should be mindful, however, of the difference between freedom and autonomy. To be left alone is to have autonomy. And as long as we do what we're told or pose no threat to those in power, we can have a lot of autonomy. If you do as you're told and make no challenging demands, your boss will be happy to leave you alone. So will most government leaders. After all, it saves energy if you are willing to police yourself. But this is hardly freedom.

To have freedom is to be able to formulate options, not just to choose from the ones we're given. To have freedom, in this sense, we must work with others to create new ways of doing things together and thus new possibilities for living good lives. Those who benefit from arrangements of inequality will not like this. Only by being sociologically mindful can we see how to resist their power to forestall change and how to create among ourselves the power to bring new arrangements into being.

RELATED READINGS

Bartky, Sandra. (1990). *Femininity and Domination*. New York: Routledge.

Domhoff, G. William. (1990). *The Power Elite and the State: How Policy Is Made in America*. New York: Aldine.

Dye, Thomas. (1995). *Who's Running America? The Clinton Years* (6th ed.). Englewood Cliffs, NJ: Prentice-Hall.

Lukes, Steven. (1974). *Power: A Radical View*. London: Macmillan.

Parenti, Michael. (1978). *Power and the Powerless*. New York: St. Martin's.

Wrong, Dennis. (1988). *Power: Its Forms, Bases, and Uses*. Chicago: University of Chicago Press.

CHAPTER ELEVEN

How to Tell Differences from Inequalities

One time, during a discussion of inequality, I said that people with more money and education tend to have different values and tastes than people with less money and education. This was a minor point that I didn't expect to cause any trouble. But a young woman came to me after class with a worried look. "Don't you think it's good to celebrate diversity?" she asked, surprising me with the question. "Well, I suppose, maybe. Diversity in what?" I said. "Like in tastes and values," she said. "You know, like you said go along with social class." It seemed that she had taken my point to be that the values and tastes of the rich were better than those of the poor. I said that that was not at all what I meant.

As we talked, I realized why this student had misunderstood me. She wanted to see social class differences as similar to ethnic differences. If people talked and dressed and ate and carried on differently because they had different levels of income and education, this was, she believed, an interesting and desirable condition. I said that things were more complicated and that we had better come back to this at the start of the next class.

During the next class we talked about the kinds of differences that exist between people. We talked about how some differences make society more interesting—for example, different styles in clothing, food, music, literature, dance, art, and language. We talked about how other differences, such as in religious beliefs, political values, or sexual preferences, can be threatening and disruptive, especially if people are intolerant and lack compassion. Then we came back to social class, and again some students wanted to see it as just another interesting kind of difference.

I said that social class was not simply a matter of difference but of harmful inequality. Why, I asked, would we want to celebrate the fact that some people work at hard, dirty, dangerous jobs for low pay while others have vastly more wealth (often through nothing more than inheritance) than they need or could ever use? Was this something to celebrate or was it a flaw in how our society worked? Certainly it was a different *kind* of difference, not like the happy differences between lefse, tortillas, rice pancakes, and crepes.

After we talked about this for a while, one student asked, "Are you saying that nothing good comes from social class differences? Isn't it good that we have a system in which some people can be free to think and to create?" These were hard questions that moved the conversation ahead by forcing us to consider things in a larger context.

Yes, I said, money could buy a fine education and give a person time to do creative work. And yes, it was good that at least some people enjoyed these possibilities. But did these possibilities *require* inequality? Surely we could educate everyone and allow time for creative work, I said, without vast inequalities in income and wealth. I also said it was important to consider the human capacities that were wasted when so many people never got to develop their talents. Perhaps with more equality, I said, we could have a richer society for everyone, because more people would have time to think, create, and care for each other.

One student pointed out that poverty and oppression had given rise to a lot of creative adaptations—ways to survive and to enjoy life—on the part of African, poor, and working-class people. He cited jazz, blues, gospel, and country music as examples. Another student replied that these were inadvertent results that came at a high cost. I agreed: Just because some people can produce great art under horrible conditions doesn't mean we ought to tolerate such conditions. I said that even under the best conditions, human life would not lack for the tension and conflict that spark creative work.

I hoped that this discussion would help students to see differences and inequalities in a sociologically mindful way. The point was that some kinds of differences are good because they give us all a chance to enjoy more kinds of food, clothing, music, and so on, but that other kinds of differences—in wealth and income, for example—are destructive. If some people can't afford to eat nutritious meals, clothe themselves against the cold, get a good education, or take time for creative work, then not only do they suffer, but the whole society suffers because the talents and energies of some of its members are lost.

How, then, can we be sociologically mindful of the difference between differences and inequalities? We must ask, In what ways does this difference matter? Does the difference allow one group to benefit at the expense of another? Does it give one group power over another? Does it mean that members of one group get less respect than another? In short, we must ask, Does this difference cause harm? If a difference leads to exploitation, unfair advantage, domination, or some other kind of harm, then it is more than a difference. It is a form of inequality and not worth celebrating.

Forms of Inequality

An inequality exists when a difference between people or between groups benefits one person or one group relative to another. That seems clear enough. But it is still a slippery idea, since it doesn't say what counts as a benefit. Perhaps, then, it would help to be more concrete about the forms that inequality can take in the United States. In what ways can individuals and groups be unequal, and how do these inequalities matter? Here are some possibilities:

- To start with the obvious, some people have more wealth (stocks, bonds, property) and income (salaries, wages, interest) than others. Money is a universal resource because it can be used to acquire all kinds of things that make life more comfortable, enjoyable, and stimulating. Money doesn't guarantee happiness, of course, but it is very useful for acquiring the things and experiences that foster happiness.

- Some people have more and better education than others. Education can help people make sense of the world, solve problems, avoid mistakes, articulate their ideas, appreciate history, and enjoy art, literature, music, and other cultural products. It can also be used to make connections and to get jobs.

- Some people have more prestigious jobs than others. A judge, for example, has a more prestigious job than a secretary; an engineer has a more prestigious job than a janitor. Having a prestigious job can in turn help to elicit respect from others. In U.S. culture, a person's status in a community often depends largely on the prestige of his or her job.

- Some people have more political power than others. Perhaps this comes from having money or from connections. In any case, having political power means being able to get people in government to take your problems seriously and look after your interests.

- Some people have better health than others. This isn't necessarily a natural result of physiology. It also results from better access to quality health care, from having less dangerous jobs, and from living in less polluted environments.

- Some people enjoy more safety than others. They do not have to worry about injuries on the job, being hit by stray bullets in their neighborhoods, or being unable to afford new tires and brakes for their cars.

- Some people have more access to art, films, theater, concerts, and other cultural events than others. Not everyone wants to go to the opera or to browse in art galleries. Even so, many people who might enjoy such activities never get a chance to take them in.

- Some people can afford to travel widely, while others cannot. Seeing other countries, meeting different kinds of people, and experiencing other cultures can be enjoyable and stimulating. Many people cannot afford these experiences.

- Some people can afford luxurious homes, some can afford decent homes, some can afford small homes, some can barely afford to rent, and others cannot afford housing at all. Not having a quiet, safe, private space in which to relax can make it hard to recover from the stresses of everyday life.

- Some people can afford to eat the most delicious, artfully prepared food, while others must make do with whatever they can scrape together. Even simple health food (organically grown fruits and vegetables, for example) can be more expensive than the heavily processed food sold in discount grocery stores. Eating well and eating healthily are thus out of the reach of some people.

- Some people can afford well-made, durable, and stylish clothes. Others must buy clothes of lesser quality, clothes that are also a sign of having less money. Some people can thus feel exposed by the clothes they wear, even while others can use clothes to flaunt their wealth.

- Some people have better and more powerful tools than others—not just hand tools or power tools, but all kinds of tools for making things happen. A printing press is a tool; so is a computer; so is an aircraft carrier.

- Some people have more information than others. Information is a resource that can help people make good plans, avoid being manipulated, and get what they want. To lack information is to be at the mercy of a world that seems to operate in a mysterious way.

- Some people have better networks than others. By "networks" I mean connections to supportive friends, helpful mentors, knowledgeable teachers, and acquaintances who can help make further connections. A better network isn't necessarily a bigger one, but one in which there are more people who already possess, and are willing to share, useful resources, such as money, tools, information, and so on.

- Some people have more skill and more control over their work than others. To have skill is to possess a resource that can be traded for a decent wage or salary. It is also to have a kind of power to make things happen. Having control over one's work is also more satisfying than being closely supervised and always told what to do and how to do it.

These are not the only forms that inequality takes in U.S. society. Perhaps you can think of others. In each case the inequality means that some people have advantages over others—more specifically, they have better chances to live good lives. Part of being sociologically mindful is seeing these differences and recognizing how they matter.

Perhaps you can also see that advantages tend to accumulate. For example, people with a great deal of wealth and income can turn these resources into other things: comfort, safety, security, pleasure, political power, excitement, information, networks, and so on. These things, in turn, might add to a person's ability to accumulate more wealth. Similarly, the lack of a key resource—education, for example—can make it hard to get more of other resources.

We should also be mindful that these inequalities are social, not personal. They are social because they result from how society is organized and where people fit into that pattern of organization. For example, one can be born into poverty only in a society that allows poverty to exist. Likewise, one can feel lucky to have a clean, safe, high-paying job only in a society where many people are forced to take dirty, unsafe, low-paying jobs.

To say that society is rife with inequalities is not to say that everyone who is disadvantaged lives in constant misery. Hardship is not pleasant, of course; nor is injustice. Yet many people who do not have much money or formal education, do not travel, do not have luxurious homes or go to fancy restaurants . . . are happy. This is not terribly surprising. Human beings are resourceful and can adapt to all kinds of conditions. Once basic needs for food, clothing, shelter, and companionship are met, humans are adept at creating ways to comfort themselves and wring happiness out of simple things.

In light of this, some people might say, "You see? These folks are happy with simple things. They don't need much. They don't even know what they're missing, so there's really no need to get upset about our wealth. It is a source of happiness for us and yet takes nothing away from our inferiors. In fact, they should be grateful that we keep them busy with productive work. Now why disrupt a system that works so well?"

Statements like this have been used in many times and places (e.g., in the U.S. South during slavery times) to justify the misery suffered by working people. The premise of this justification is that some human beings are not worth as much as others. If that premise is accepted, then it becomes only logical to use the time, bodies, and energy of inferior people to create happiness for those who are better. This sort of thinking helps perpetuate inequality by allowing some people to believe that they are entitled to live well at the expense of others.

Invisible Resources

There is a bumper sticker that says, "Dress for Success—Wear a White Penis." This wry slogan reminds us not only that white males have, on the average, better chances of success in a society run by white males, but that people in other groups can't shed their disadvantages as easily as changing clothes. If the bumper sticker makes us laugh, it is because we know that as a piece of advice it is absurd; if you are not born with a white penis, it is almost impossible to put one on, at least in any convincing way.

Being sociologically mindful, we can see another point: Differences between bodies are not mere differences if one kind of body can elicit more respect than another. For example, in a society where things male and masculine are more highly valued than things female and feminine, a male body is a more valuable resource than a female body. If you dwell in a male body, you are more likely to be listened to, taken seriously, and seen as a potential leader. You can always end up proving yourself to be a fool, but at the start you will be given the benefit of the doubt because of your body.

Similarly, in a society where European features, especially light skin, straight hair, and a sleek nose, are more highly valued—or seen as "beautiful"—then possessing a body with these features is a plus. With these features, you may be seen as having more innate goodness and intelligence and thus be treated better. And if those who are already in power see you as looking like they do, they may be more inclined to admit you to their circles, thus giving you access to further resources.

The heading of this section suggests that skin tone and body type are somehow "invisible" resources. How can this be? Don't these resources have to be visible to produce results? The answer has to do with who sees what. It often happens that those who possess features that are more highly valued do not see the advantages these features provide. It is as if a person were blind to a badge s/he was wearing.

White people, for example, often fail to see that merely having light skin means they will be treated better in many situations than people with dark skin and African features. Being "treated better" means being listened to, appreciated as an individual, presumed competent or trustworthy, and recognized as entitled to dignity and respect. You might think, "What's so special about this? This is how it should be for everyone." You are right, of course, but this is not how things are for everyone. That, too, can be hard to see.

Having a male body can work the same way. All else being equal, a person in a male body is more likely to be presumed credible and capable. It is as if the male body were a sign that said, "Be assured that I know what I'm talking about and can back up my talk with action." And yet, as with whites and skin color, males seldom see that their bodies bring them unearned advantages *relative to women*. The full value of a male body as a resource thus remains invisible to those who possess it.

Bodies can also possess other kinds of resources that are invisible until used. For example, strength, coordination, and muscle control are bodily resources. So is resistance to heat, cold, and disease. We could also include acute hearing, sight, smell, taste, and touch. All of these capacities reside in the body, as a result of natural endowments and training, and we might not know that a person possesses these resources until they are displayed.

Are such bodily resources differences or inequalities? Both. A difference in strength, for example, is, by definition, an inequality because it means that one person is stronger than another. What matters, however, is whether strength can be used to produce other kinds of inequalities. If people could legally enslave others who were weaker, then strength would be quite an asset. Likewise, if people were paid according to how much heavy lifting they could do, strength could be turned into inequality in wealth. So we must be mindful that what counts as a resource depends on the situation.

Visible Origins of Invisible Resources

Where do invisible resources come from? Even strength, which at first seems like a genetic matter, is affected by culture and experience. Without proper nutrition and exercise, people who are destined to grow tall and wide do not necessarily become very strong. And even small people can develop their strength to the point where it exceeds that of others who are twice as big. Much can happen, by choice or by accident, to shape our bodies in certain ways and not others.

Other kinds of resources that reside in the body depend even more on experience and training. No matter what our potential might be, we always depend on others to teach us how to do things, to give us problems to solve, and to help us correct our mistakes. Differences in skill and problem-solving ability (what some people call "intelligence") thus arise out of social life. We like to be rewarded for what our bodies and minds can do. Unfortunately, many people never get the chance to learn to do what is valued by those who can dole out rewards.

We can see that social experience conditions our bodies to react to the world in certain ways. Suppose you looked up from the page right now and saw a wizened old man with bulging eyes and flecks of spittle on his chin coming at you with a knife in one hand and a rattlesnake in the other. What would you do? You might shriek, freeze, run, cower, or throw this book at him. In any case, you would surely have a bodily reaction—your heart would pound, your chest would tighten—and this reaction would be a result of how your body has been conditioned to respond to scenes you interpret as threatening.

This odd example serves to illustrate the point that our bodies, not only our minds, react to the world in ways that result from how we have been conditioned to react. Recognizing that these responses are conditioned is important, for it reminds us that we do not control all our reactions to the world. What is important to see is that some ways of responding to the world are more valued, and more useful, than others and more likely to lead to inequality.

Imagine that you are invited to give a public talk about sociological mindfulness. The talk should be about an hour long and is set for a week from today. Your family, friends, and teachers will be there, along with most of the leaders of the community in which you live. You can expect an audience of about 1,500 people, not counting reporters and photographers. When you speak, you will be representing not only yourself but all the people and groups to which you belong. If you do well, you will receive more honors and probably several job offers.

The prospect of giving such a talk would make many people extremely anxious. They would worry about looking unpoised, about saying the wrong thing, about embarrassing themselves and others. A person who reacted this way might think, "I am so nervous I can't think straight. I can't prepare adequately in just a week! I know I am going to blow it. My heart pounds when I imagine getting up in front of all those people. I can't do this!" This sort of reaction might make it hard to do a good job, thus leading to the bad performance that is so feared.

Another person chosen to give the same talk might say, "Thank you for this honor. A week will be plenty of time to prepare. I'll get to work right away and do my best." Then, brimming with self-confidence, this person brushes up on sociological mindfulness and studies the speeches of great orators throughout history. S/he then writes a first draft, revises it, gets comments from others, revises it again, practices giving the talk, revises some more, and then finally, on the big day, does a great job, makes everyone proud, and launches a brilliant career.

Why might two people react so differently to the prospect of giving a public talk? It is not much help to say, "Some people are more comfortable speaking in public than others." That is an observation, not an explanation.

Being sociologically mindful we would ask, What *experiences* led one person to be so confident and the other to be so anxious and afraid? How did one person *learn* to have faith in his or her abilities, and the other person not? We would try to understand how it happened that these people learned to feel so differently about their abilities and about the challenge of using them.

We should also be mindful that ways of responding to the world, the ways that are conditioned into us, are patterned. Some types of people are more likely to be conditioned to respond to problems with calm faith in their own abilities and worth. If you are white, male, and upper middle class, you will probably have more experiences that nurture your talents, affirm your sense of worth as a person, and give you confidence that you can do whatever you set your mind to than if you are a black woman growing up in poverty.

Obviously this is not true in every case. Some white men from rich families can be plagued by self-doubt. And there are many women of color, from all kinds of backgrounds, whose families and communities instill in them tremendous abilities and pride. Yet on the whole, on the average, the pattern holds, as it must, in a society that is run by and privileges whites, males, and those with wealth. In general, those who are born with more visible resources have better chances of acquiring the inner resources that lead to further advantages.

Reconditioning Ourselves

Upon hearing this argument about inner resources, a student said, "But isn't this a lot like in nature? You know, those who survive and succeed are the fittest—the ones who are, for whatever reason, best adapted to the environment." I said yes, the situation could be seen that way, but that there are two differences.

One difference is that in nature, creatures are what they are by virtue of genetic endowment; they do not become what they are by going to school, learning skills, and acquiring the habits and dispositions that allow them to survive. In the social world, however, we must devote conscious effort to all the tasks needed to turn children into fully functioning, talented adults. If we don't do this, human beings can be damaged or stunted.

The second way things are different with humans, I said, is that our environment is not simply given to us by nature but is socially constructed. The survival-of-the-fittest analogy is thus wrong, because the social world *can* be changed to make it safe and nurturing for all kinds of people. We do not have to sacrifice human beings as if they were little fish deserving to be eaten by bigger fish. That kind of predatory arrangement does not make for a very humane world.

Reconditioning ourselves is always a possibility. If a lack of self-confidence is the problem, we can practice setting achievable goals and then work to achieve them, thus boosting our self-confidence. We can also learn new skills, habits, and ideas at any time. This becomes more difficult, of course, as we get older and settle into comfortable ruts. It might also be that others whose ruts run parallel to ours will resist our efforts to change.

Yet with support from others, remarkable change remains possible. If our relationships with others make us what we are, then we can potentially remake ourselves by relating differently to others, or by forming relationships with different others. As long as there exists the possibility of doing this, of making these kinds of changes, we need not resign ourselves to accepting everything that has been instilled in us by a particular form of social life. We can always pursue growth and change in directions of our own choosing.

Being sociologically mindful, we can see how certain highly visible facts of social life—such as huge inequalities in wealth, status, and power—can lead to inequalities in the distribution of invisible resources. The old adage "To them that have shall be given" is a poetic way of making the same point, which is that advantages tend to accumulate. If we are mindful of the bad results that arise from this tendency, we can decide to reorganize ourselves to make things turn out differently, with greater justice for all.

False Parallels

One time I was talking about how women are hurt by occupational segregation, which is the practice of steering women into jobs that pay less than "men's jobs." A man in the class said, "Men are hurt by occupational segregation, too." When I asked how, he explained that he wanted to become an elementary school teacher but that, as a man, he had been discouraged from doing so. He argued that just as women are oppressed if they are directed away from high-paying "men's jobs" (e.g., engineer, surgeon), he was oppressed because his wish to be an elementary school teacher was not being honored.

His statement evoked a great deal of sympathy. Most people in the class seemed to agree that there was something unfair about his being discouraged from being an elementary school teacher, a job that is usually held by women. His example implied that occupational segregation was equally bad for women and men. He was suggesting that women did not have it any worse than men, because men experienced parallel problems.

I asked the young man who was discouraging him. "My dad and my uncles," he said. I asked if he was being discouraged by anyone in the university or in the public school system. "No, if anything they want more men to go into elementary education," he said. I asked why, if the future for men in elementary education looked so bright, his dad and uncles were discouraging him. "They say it's a woman's job, and that I could do better," he said. At that point the parallel broke down.

This young man's experience was *not* like what women experience when they seek jobs typically held by men. In seeking to become an elementary school teacher, this young man wasn't being told, "You are not good enough for this kind of job." He was being told, "This job is not good enough for you." But even this message did not come from anyone with any power to keep him out. It was his dad and uncles who said he was setting his sights too low. A young woman who wanted to become an engineer or a surgeon would probably not get that sort of message.

Despite all this, I urged the young man to stick to his goals if he wanted to teach children. Then he said, "It's not so much that I want to teach children. I figured I'd teach for a few years and then go into administration. A lot of school systems are eager to hire men as elementary-school principals, and from there you can go on to be a superintendent." I was disappointed to hear him say this. The young man who claimed to be oppressed had in fact calculated that his gender would *aid* his career. There was no parallel here to women's experiences of exclusion from the most rewarding jobs.

Taking History and Context into Account

Another false parallel often comes up when talking about racism. If I talk about white racism, someone will invariably say, "Yeah, but blacks can be racist, too." I ask how that can be, and someone will explain: "You see it all the time. Like in the cafeteria. Blacks sit by themselves and exclude white students. They also make disparaging remarks about whites, just like some whites do about blacks. That's racism." Actually, while this behavior might reflect prejudice, it is not racism. Being sociologically mindful, we can see why accusing blacks of racism— for keeping to themselves or for satirizing whites—is a false parallel.

Part of being sociologically mindful is taking history and context into account. If we do that, we can see two things. One is that it was not Africans but Europeans who invented the racial categories "black" and "white" to justify colonization and slavery. If any group is racist, it is the group that invents and imposes such categories. It makes no sense to call the victims racist.

We can also see that in the United States blacks have never had the power to oppress or exploit whites; nor have whites had to suffer daily indignities at the hands of a black majority. When it comes to oppression, exploitation, and disrespect, the situation has been, and remains, entirely the other way around. Blacks have suffered, not benefited, from the idea of "race" and the social arrangements built on this idea.

So if blacks, who are still a relatively powerless minority in the United States, disparage whites and try to maintain solidarity among themselves, this is not racism but *resistance* to racism. To say that blacks who are unfriendly to whites or who tell jokes about whites are "just as racist" as whites who do the same things to blacks is a false parallel. It is false because it ignores the historical responsibility for racism; it ignores the huge differences in power between blacks and whites; and it ignores the different consequences that arise, depending on who is disparaging whom.

Anyone can exhibit prejudice if they embrace stereotypes about members of another group. And so if some blacks see all whites as untrustworthy bigots, we can call this "being prejudiced." Understandably, many white people resent this stereotype. But since blacks as a group do not have the power to discriminate against whites, any prejudice harbored by blacks is of little consequence. Without power it is simply impossible to "do racism." Being sociologically mindful, we can see that doing racism requires not only prejudice but also the *power to discriminate* in ways that hurt others.

Often I can make this point about power and discrimination by asking how many students believe that to get their first big job they will have to please a black employer. So far no one has raised a hand when I've asked that question. I then ask how many students believe that their career success will depend on the judgments of black employers. Again, no hands.

The difference in power between racial groups in the United States also suggests why it is a false parallel to say that when blacks exclude whites from their gatherings, this is the same as whites excluding blacks. If whites hold most positions of power, and tend to give such positions to others who are like them—others who are in their networks—then people who are excluded from these networks will suffer; they will be locked out and kept powerless. Blacks, on the other hand, have relatively little power and wealth, so if they say, "We prefer not to associate with people who look down on us," that is not cause for much suffering among whites.

Recall the student who mentioned blacks sitting by themselves in the cafeteria. It is curious that this example comes up so often. It's a good example of a false parallel that is made just to avoid seeing what is really going on.

I once asked a white student who cited the pattern of separate seating to explain why it bothered him. "Are you bothered because you want to sit at a table with your black friends and suddenly, when they're together, they don't want you to join them?" I asked. He said no, that wasn't it; he said that the black students he was thinking of weren't even his friends. So I asked, "If they aren't your friends, why do you want to sit with them?"

While he was thinking, a black woman raised her hand and said, "People sit with their friends if there's room. It's just that white students are more likely to have white friends and black students more likely to have black friends." She was trying to make peace.

Then another black woman said, "It isn't that white students want to sit with us. It's that whites are so used to being able to go wherever they want and sit wherever they want, they resent it if there's even one place where they don't feel free to go." All of the black students and about half of the whites nodded their heads in agreement. It seemed that she had hit the nail on the head.

False Gender Parallels

In discussing the problem of sexual violence, I try to make the point that part of the problem (one of the enabling conditions) is men's practice of sexually objectifying women. This refers to men talking about and treating women as targets of sexual conquest rather than as human beings. When I make this point, often someone will say, "Yes, but women also sexually objectify men. Women talk about men as 'hunks,' and remember there was that television commercial where the secretaries ogled the male construction worker."

To equate women's sexual objectification of men with men's sexual objectification of women is false for two reasons. One is that men do it more often, because showing sexual interest in women—showing that you are attracted to their bodies as sexual objects—is part of signifying (heterosexual) manhood in U.S. culture. The more important reason is that the consequences of objectification are different in the two cases, because men have greater power to harm women physically and economically.

A woman who is treated as a sexual object is not being respected as a complete human being. It is this lesser respect for a woman's personhood that underlies rape and other forms of sexual coercion. It also underlies discrimination in the workplace (it is hard to appreciate the intellect and skill of a person who is perceived as a set of body parts). Again, it is men who, because of their physical strength and institutional power, can cause harm to women—harm that grows out of treating others as objects. Women generally do not have the power to harm men, so the sexual objectification in which women engage is rarely a threat to any man's body, status, or career.

Being sociologically mindful does not lead to the conclusion that it's wrong for men to objectify women but okay if women do it to men. To objectify others is wrong because it is likely to produce harm, if only by reinforcing the habit of ignoring the humanity of other people. We must be mindful, however, of how the consequences of objectification can be very different, depending on who is objectifying whom, under what conditions. When there is a serious imbalance in power, and especially the power to cause harm, we must take this imbalance into account and not let a false parallel keep us from seeing which acts of objectification are more dangerous and damaging.

Patterns in True Parallels

One time I was talking about death rates from stress-related diseases, such as heart attacks, strokes, and liver failure. I pointed out that the rates were higher for black men and for working-class men than for white men and middle-class men. In response, a student said, "But there are a lot of executives who have stress-related health problems, too." I said that while this was true, the data on death rates contained a more important lesson: Inequality in U.S. society is one reason that some men, those on the lower end of the economic ladder, die sooner than others.

Instead of grasping this lesson, the student tried to conjure a parallel, as if to say, "Sure, workers have their health troubles, but then so do executives." While this is not literally false, to put matters this way distorts reality. If executives are stressed, it is often because they are trying to hold onto power; when workers are stressed, it is often because they lack power. Invoking a parallel between workers and executives also implies that both groups suffer equally—a notion that is clearly false, as shown by the differences in death rates.

Being sociologically mindful does not mean ignoring all parallels. In fact, it is good to look for them, since true parallels can reveal important things about how the social world works. Perhaps, for example, there is a commonality in the troubles experienced by working-class *men* and executive *men*. Both groups of men might be striving, in parallel ways, for control over their lives. This would be worth looking into. Still, we should not presume that a parallel, even if it is a true parallel, is necessarily an equivalence.

Being sociologically mindful does not mean ignoring the troubles of people in privileged groups; nor does it mean overlooking the misbehavior of people in oppressed groups. Being mindful means paying attention to context, to history, and to power, so that we can see when differences are inequalities, and when false parallels make inequalities seem to disappear.

Self-Justification and a Test for Justice

We could say that people make false parallels, refuse to see inequalities, or try to portray inequalities as mere differences because they are not being sociologically mindful. But what is behind the resistance to being mindful in these matters? Perhaps it is a desire to justify one's place in the world. People who enjoy privileges because of their race, gender, income, or sexuality usually seek to justify the arrangements that provide these privileges.

It is hard to change people's thinking when their view of the social world also supports a favorable view of themselves. Someone who has status, wealth, and power is likely to embrace a view of society as a place of fair and open competition, since this view implies that they have done well through their own merits. A critical view of society might threaten this view of themselves. Nor is it very useful to say, "Think harder, stop deluding yourself, and face up to reality." Most privileged people will respond by thinking harder about how to justify holding onto the version of reality they prefer.

It is possible, however, to get people to consider a different way of seeing if a way can be found to preempt their need to self-justify. How can this be done? One way I have tried to do this is with an exercise (inspired by the thinking of philosopher John Rawls) that might be called a "test for justice." It is a collective thought experiment that comes with these instructions:

A new society is in the works. The principles of distributive justice on which this new society will operate remain to be formulated. Your job is to formulate them. You have been chosen to do this precisely because you don't know anything else about this new society. More importantly, you don't know what your place in this new society is going to be. Thus you are perfectly situated to come up with principles that will produce a fair distribution of wealth, since you can't know how to tilt the game to your advantage. Your task, then, is to do the following:

1. Formulate the rule or rules by which it will be determined who gets how much wealth in this new society.

2. Formulate the rule or rules by which it will be determined what each person must contribute to this new society.

3. Show how the rules you formulate will maximize justice and equality. (Obviously, you need to define what you mean by "justice" and "equality.") Be sure to consider how your rules will produce fair results even in unusual cases.

This is a difficult exercise for most people. For one thing, it is hard to imagine not knowing who we would be in a new society, since we are so used to being who we are. For another thing, we are unused to anyone asking us how to distribute wealth in a just way. Yet the basic idea behind the exercise is simple: *If you don't know what your position will be in this new society, you have no privileges to justify and every reason to devise rules that will ensure justice for everyone.*

Here are some of the rules that my students and others have proposed for determining who gets how much wealth: (i) everybody gets a share of wealth that is in proportion to what they contribute to society; (ii) everybody gets exactly the same equal share of society's collective wealth; (iii) everybody gets whatever amount of wealth they need to live a decent life, plus some extra if they have special hardships.

Some of these rules don't work so well when we get to the third part of the exercise because what at first glance seems fair—such as distributing wealth based on contributions to society—can produce unfair results in many cases, such as when people are disabled and can't do as much work as others. Even the strict equality rule—everybody gets an equal share of the wealth—runs into trouble because some people (e.g., those raising several children) have greater needs than others (e.g., those who are single, with no dependents). To give everyone an equal share would thus produce an unjust result because some people would get more than they need, while others would get less than they need.

It is interesting to see the problems that arise when trying to formulate a rule for determining what each person must contribute to the new society. You might wonder why such a rule is necessary. For one thing, every society depends on people doing what is necessary to keep the society going. Someone has to grow and sell food, build houses, clean up, care for children, and do thousands of other unglamorous tasks. No society could last if everyone decided to sit back and live off the fruits of other people's labors.

Another reason for formulating a rule about contributions is to ensure fairness in the new society. No one should have to do more than their share of the necessary labor, and no one (who is able to work) should get away with a free ride. So what kind of rule can we devise to ensure that fairness prevails? Here is one possibility: We will calculate how much time it takes to do all the work necessary to keep society going and then divide up this work equally among all who are able to work. Perhaps it will turn out that we need 20 hours a week from everyone to keep society running. If so, then the rule becomes "everyone must put in their 20 hours a week."

A rule like this is just a starting point; we would still have to figure out who gets to do what kind of work. Many people might say, "I'll do my 20 hours a week as a brain surgeon because that seems most interesting." Probably too few people would say, "I'll put in my 20 hours as a garbage collector because I like stench and filth." We would thus have to come up with a rule to deal with inequalities in different types of work, to make sure that pleasant work and unpleasant work were fairly distributed. Perhaps we would need a rule like this: Everyone must do a share of the dirty work; no one gets to do fun and interesting work all the time; and no one gets stuck doing dirty work all the time.

There are many possible rules, all of which solve some problems of justice while creating others. But that is inevitable; we always have to keep thinking about how to make sure that our abstract rules, principles, and guidelines lead to good results in concrete circumstances. That is in large part what human intelligence is for. Being sociologically mindful means bringing this intelligence to bear on problems in the social world.

The goal of the test-for-justice exercise is not to arrive at a single vision of what a just society would look like. The goal is to encourage thinking and conversation about justice and about how well our current society produces just or unjust results. This exercise seems to make it easier for people to see problems in existing society because they do not get so caught up in justifying arrangements that benefit them. Instead they think about the kinds of arrangements that would produce better results for everyone.

I have also noticed that one idea never comes up during this exercise. No one has ever said, "To maximize justice and equality, all we need to do is use the same rules that govern U.S. society right now." No one says this, I think, because once the incentive for self-justification is gone, they are free to be more sociologically mindful than usual.

RELATED READINGS

Frye, Marilyn. (1983). "Oppression." Pp. 1–16 in *The Politics of Reality*. Freedom, CA: Crossing Press.

Hacker, Andrew. (1992). *Two Nations: Black and White, Separate, Hostile, Unequal*. New York: Charles Scribner's Sons.

Hurst, Charles. (1992). *Social Inequality: Forms, Causes, and Consequences*. Boston: Allyn and Bacon.

McIntosh, Peggy. (1997). "White Privilege and Male Privilege: A Personal Account of Coming to See Correspondences through Work in Women's Studies." Pp. 76–87 in Margaret Anderson and Patricia Hill Collins (eds.), *Race, Class, and Gender: An Anthology*. Belmont, CA: Wadsworth.

Rawls, John. (1971). *A Theory of Justice*. Cambridge, MA: Harvard University Press.

Williams, Christine. (1992). "The Glass Escalator: Hidden Advantages for Men in the 'Female' Professions." *Social Problems* 39:253–267.

Wright, Erik O., Costello, C., Hachen, D., & Sprague, J. (1982). "The American Class Structure." *American Sociological Review* 47:709–726.

CHAPTER TWELVE

Finding Out How the Social World Works

If I said that the central processor in my computer is not a silicon chip but a positronic wafer that operates at 10^3 gigahertz by sending modulated gravimetric pulses through a high-density tachyon field at twice the speed of light, you might not know whether to believe me. Perhaps this sounds plausible. After all, do you really know what goes on inside a computer? Maybe I'm just bragging about my fancy computer by spouting jargon that is unfamiliar to you.

If you know anything about physics, however, you know that my computer story is silly. The reference to things traveling "at twice the speed of light" gives away the joke. Even if you didn't know that the speed of light is unexceedable, but you knew a little about computers and kept up with the news, you could still guess that the story is outrageous, since it is implausible that "positronic wafers," "gravimetric pulses," "high-density tachyon fields," and a processor operating at "10^3 gigahertz" somehow ended up in a home computer without being widely reported.

This example shows how we can know things through deduction. You had to know only one fact—that nothing can go faster than the speed of light—to deduce that my story about the positronic wafer was nonsense. Or you might have known that powerful computing technologies do not first appear in home computers. In any case, the point is that by knowing one thing, or just a few things, and then reasoning carefully, we can arrive at conclusions that help us sort sense from nonsense.

Here is another example. Without looking up any statistics, can you say whether there are more poor black people or poor white people in the United States? A common mistake, because blacks are often represented as being poor, is to say that there are more poor black people than poor white people. But blacks make up only about 12 percent of the U.S. population. And even though the rate of poverty is higher among blacks (about 30%) than among whites (about 15%), there are so many more white people in the United States that whites still make up the majority of those living in poverty. Again, a few facts and a bit of logic make this easy to figure out.

So logical deduction is one way to know things, or to find out the implications of what we know. Much of what we know comes straight from others. It is passed on to us by parents, teachers, friends, and so on. We can also know things from personal experience or observation, from systematic research, and from mystical revelation. It is possible, too, that some knowledge is instinctive, as, for example, when an infant "knows" that it should suck on whatever is put in its mouth.

It is interesting to think about where our knowledge comes from. What usually concerns us more, however, is how to be sure that our knowledge is valid and reliable. Each source of knowledge has limitations in these respects. Part of being sociologically mindful is being aware of these limitations.

Logical deduction, for instance, is a fine way to elaborate our knowledge—except that if our *premises* are wrong, then our conclusions will also be wrong; we will simply reason our way to further ignorance. One strength of logical deduction, however, is that others can check up on our assumptions and our reasoning, and thus correct us if we go astray.

Relying on what others tell us is necessary and is often a good way to learn, but how do we know that what others tell us is right? Surely you have had the experience of being told—by a parent, teacher, or mentor—something that later turned out to be wrong. Then there is the problem of deciding between different versions of the truth that come to us from sources that seem equally credible. How do we decide who is right?

Personal experience and observation are good sources of knowledge, except that it is easy to misjudge and overgeneralize from these sources. For example, your own observations might tell you that the sun revolves around the earth, or that all Lithuanians are slobs because both of the Lithuanians you've met in your life were a bit slobby, or that there is no ruling class in the United States because you've never seen it gathered in one place, or that crime is rising because you were just robbed. The problem in each case is not that you don't know what you've seen, but that what you've seen isn't enough to support the conclusion you reached.

As for mystical revelation, it is perhaps a way to gain spiritual knowledge for one's self, but it is not a good way to learn about the social world, since there is no way for others to check up on or to refute another person's mystical revelations. If you claimed to know—because the notion just popped into your head—that this book is a tool of the devil, how could I disagree? I suppose I could say that I had a mystical revelation myself and, on this basis, I know that this book is a gift from Hermes—and you should believe me because, after all, it is my book. But this would be a very strange and irresolvable argument to get into.

Advantages of Systematic Research

Careful research is perhaps the best way to create valid and reliable knowledge about the state of the social world and how it works. It is the best way for several reasons. First, by using standard, widely accepted means of finding things out, we can control personal biases. If we can do this, we are less likely to mistake what we would like to be true for what is really true.

Suppose, for example, I believe that democratic work organizations are better than authoritarian ones and would therefore like to believe that they are also more efficient. My bias would be to look only for evidence that supports my belief. But if I use a standard method of assessing efficiency, and use it carefully and fairly to compare democratic and authoritarian work organizations, I will have to accept whatever I find. My bias would thus be canceled out, or at least controlled.

Second, research can get us beyond personal experience and casual observation, because to re-*search* is to look beyond what is obvious to us from where we stand. It is to look for ideas and information that might challenge the common sense that gets us through daily life. It means considering the quality and correctness of knowledge created by others, even if we find their knowledge irritating. All this can be difficult, because our usual habit is to settle comfortably into believing that we already know what is right.

A third reason for doing research it that it lets us check up on each other. If we use methods that others agree are proper, they can look at our results and say, "Hmmm, yes, you did it right; these results must be correct." Or they can say, "Ah, you went astray here at this point, so your conclusions are not trustworthy." We can make the same judgments when others offer us knowledge they have created. In this way, by working together, we can do better at dispelling illusions and, in the long run, creating knowledge that is valid and reliable.

Perhaps you noticed that I had only good things to say about knowledge that comes from research. Does this mean that one should accept as true whatever is published in a scientific or scholarly journal? No. Knowledge from any source should be critically interrogated. Careful research is just a way to avoid problems that are common when knowledge is created in other ways. And if research is not done properly, it can yield as much foolishness as any other method.

The larger point here is that we should be mindful, to the extent we can, of where our own knowledge comes from. We can be mindful in this way by asking ourselves how we know what we claim to know. Is some piece of knowledge a result of logical deduction? (If so, have we reasoned correctly? How do we know that our premises are correct?) Is some piece of knowledge a hand-me-down from others? (If so, where did *their* knowledge come from? How can we be sure it is correct?) Is some piece of knowledge a result of personal experience or observation? (If so, are we claiming to know more than our personal experience can warrant? Is it possible that we have observed only what we want to believe is true, or that our observations have been limited in some crucial way?)

The point of asking ourselves these questions is not to arrive at a paralyzing state of doubt about what we know, but to more wisely decide how much faith to put in what we know. If we can do this, we can open ourselves to new knowledge without fear of surrendering our minds to yet another fishy belief system. Being sociologically mindful, we can get a better view of what is coming at us by way of new knowledge and where it is coming from. We can also see what is worth catching.

The Kinds of Questions We Can Ask

All attempts to create knowledge are responses to questions, and knowledge must be created in a way that suits the question. For example, if you asked, "How much does this book weigh?" the proper way to get an answer is to weigh it. How many words does it contain?

Count them. Will it fly like a boomerang? Give it the right kind of throw and observe the result. These are *empirical* questions, which means that they are answerable by measuring, counting, or looking to see what happens.

But suppose you asked, "Is the cover of this book beautiful?" What then? You could ask ten artists for their opinions. What if seven said it was ugly, two were ambivalent, and one thought it was beautiful? In this case no measuring stick will settle the matter, because you have asked an *aesthetic* question—a question about what is subjectively pleasing to the senses—and aesthetic questions are not answerable with data. We can try to say why something strikes us as ugly or beautiful, tasteful or crass, but no evidence or logic will prove us right and others wrong.

Here is another kind of question: Was it worthwhile for me to write this book, considering that I might have been doing other useful things with my time? Again, this is not an empirical question, since there is no way to get an answer by measuring, counting, or observing. It is a *moral* question, since it calls for a judgment about what is right to do. I could say why it seemed to me a good thing to write this book, but my reasons would be based on moral precepts and on my sense of how the future is likely to unfold. There is no data I can show, no standard analysis, to prove that my answer is right. All I can do is to offer reasonable arguments.

There are also questions of *interpretation,* the most simple of which is, "What does this thing mean?" Such questions often arise when we confront works of art. We might look at a painting or read a novel and wonder what the writer or artist wanted us to understand. But any fact, object, gesture, phrase, or behavior—anything that has meaning—can raise a question of interpretation.

Sometimes we can get an answer by asking for clarification. Perhaps the writer or artist can tell us what s/he meant (although writers and artists can't always fully explain what their work means). Or perhaps there is expert opinion available to help us make sense of things. Other times there might be so much ambiguity that no clear interpretation can be nailed down. All anyone can do then is to give reasons to support the plausibility of a particular interpretation.

You can perhaps see now that research is better suited to answering some questions than others. It is a good way to answer empirical questions. It can also be useful for answering interpretive questions, because we can sometimes dig up evidence that supports the plausibility of an interpretation. And although it is wise to search for ideas and information to help guide our moral and aesthetic judgments, research will not tell us which judgments are correct.

It is good to be mindful of the kind of question we are facing. Sometimes we get into fruitless debates because we are not clear about this. There is no point, for example, in trading opinions about the correct answer to a simple empirical question. Are crime rates rising? Go to the library and look up the best answer you can find. If it is the answer to an empirical question that is in dispute, we should stop disputing and go get the answer.

Interpreting the Answers to Empirical Questions

Sometimes the answer to an empirical question can create a great deal of interpretive trouble. For example, to ask, "What are the rates of poverty among blacks and whites living in the United States?" is to ask an empirical question. We can look up the answers because someone else (the U.S. Census Bureau) has already done the counting and the arithmetic. As I noted earlier, the poverty rate among blacks is about 30 percent and among whites it is about 15 percent (these figures fluctuate somewhat and can also vary depending on how poverty is defined). But what do these figures mean? How can we interpret them?

I once presented these figures during a discussion of racial inequality. The class suddenly got quiet. No one wanted to comment on the meaning of the percentages. When I pressed for some reaction, a white student said, "I think no one is talking because the figures are embarrassing." Did he mean that the figures were embarrassing because they pointed out a failure to overcome racial inequality? I wasn't sure, so I asked him to be more explicit. "The figures are embarrassing," he said with some hesitation, "to black students." I was baffled by this.

After further conversation, it became clear that the student who spoke about the figures being "embarrassing to black students" saw the figures as evidence of black inferiority. His presumption was that the poverty rate of a group was an indicator of the capability of people in that group. I saw the figures as evidence of racism and discrimination.

In this case, the facts about poverty rates were clear, but they did not speak for themselves. The same facts lent themselves to nearly opposite interpretations.

To support my interpretation, I might have said that in the United States, millions of people, black and white, are poor because they can't find jobs that pay a decent wage, or they can't find jobs at all. Sometimes the jobs available in an area don't match people's skills. Or else the jobs disappear when employers move factories to foreign countries where they can pay workers less. And so people can end up poor, or very nearly poor, even though they are able and willing to work.

I might have added that the higher poverty rate among blacks is a result of factories being closed down in inner cities in the North, where a lot of the black population is concentrated. It's a result of schools that do not serve black children well. It's a result of discrimination in hiring and network advantages enjoyed by whites. In some cases, part of the problem is a lack of marketable skills, but that's because access to education and training is limited, not because people's natural abilities are limited.

I might have said all this—and probably did—but was it enough to establish my interpretation as correct? Although I am sure that my statement helped some people see why the white student's interpretation was wrong, others who preferred to hold onto that interpretation could point out, correctly, that I had not really *proven*—by anything I'd said or any evidence I'd shown—that blacks were not inferior to whites. All I had done was to suggest that "black inferiority" was not a plausible explanation—if other things were taken into account, if those other things were true, and if no significant counterevidence was being overlooked.

My interpretation was not, however, a matter of opinion. My interpretation was based on previously answered empirical questions. Have jobs disappeared in areas heavily populated by blacks? Do employers discriminate against blacks? Do whites enjoy network advantages when it comes to getting jobs? Do schools serve black kids as well as they serve white kids? Is there a lack of access to education and job training? With knowledge of the answers to these empirical questions, we can determine which interpretation of the poverty-rate figures is most likely to be correct.

Studying and Resolving Disagreement

Why argue about this stuff? You might think, "People are going to believe what they want to believe, and you can't convince them otherwise." Unfortunately, that is true about some people. They will not be persuaded to give up beliefs and interpretations that make them feel good about themselves. Even so, conversation can often get us to surprising places if we don't give up too soon. One thing that helps is to figure out what kind of question is bogging us down.

If the answer to an empirical question is at issue, we can say, "Neither of us knows the answer right now, but we can find one." Then we can decide whether to go on without an answer or go look one up. What we do will depend on what we are trying to understand and how important the matter is to us. Even if we don't break off a conversation and dash to the library, perhaps we will make a mental note to look something up later. That, too, is progress, since it will allow us to bring more information to a future conversation.

It is much the same when we disagree about answers to interpretive questions. What we must do, if we wish to figure out where the disagreement lies, is to try to explain the assumptions upon which our interpretations are based. This is a matter of being mindful about the ideas and beliefs upon which we draw to say what something means. If we can explain to others "where we are coming from," we are more likely to arrive at an understanding of why our interpretations differ, and how the difference might be settled.

Disagreements about aesthetic and moral questions are not easy to resolve. Some may even be impossible to resolve. Perhaps the best we can do then is to explain, as fully as possible, the grounds for preferring one answer over another. This might not lead to agreement, but it will lead to better understanding. And if we observe only one rule—to keep the conversation going—that will preclude the use of violence as a way to end a disagreement. Of course, many human beings, being less than mindful or heartful, have had great difficulty following this one rule.

Mindful Skepticism

Once, during a discussion of the benefits of education, a black woman said she was outraged to learn that, on the average, a high-school diploma was likely to yield higher earnings (by mid-life) for a white man than a college degree was likely to yield for a black woman. When she said this, another student, a white male said, "I don't believe it. How can you possibly know that?" Before she could answer, I said, "She probably read the article that was assigned for today. If you look on page 34 in the text, you'll see a table that shows what she's referring to." He paged through his book and found the table. After studying it for a few moments, he harumphed and said, "Well, anybody can make up numbers."

As a teacher, I was irritated by this response, because it meant this: "No matter what information I am presented with, if it does not suit my prior beliefs, if it does not make me comfortable, I will discount it, so I can continue to believe what I want to believe." An attitude like this leaves little room for education to make a dent. I wondered why this student would bother to study anything at all, or read any books at all, if he was so intent on being unchanged.

And yet I could not say that his attitude was entirely foolish. Numbers are often cooked up to mislead us, and numbers can be wrong because of honest mistakes, so it is reasonable to be skeptical of numbers, whatever the source. Is there any way to tell which numbers are right? Yes, it can be done; it just requires training. Since most people do not have such training, however, it is understandable that they might say, "I can't tell what's right or wrong, so I'm going to treat all statistics as hogwash."

This is clearly not a mindful response to the situation. It is like saying, "I can't read, so I am going to treat all books as hogwash." It would be better to learn to read and to learn also what is necessary to distinguish the hog from the wash. This is hard but not impossible. What helps is being mindfully, rather than indiscriminately, skeptical of new information.

One of the difficulties in learning about the social world is that we must rely on information created and filtered by others. We can't check out everything for ourselves, even if we know how. This being the case, we must pay attention to how information (in the form of words or numbers) is created, by whom, for what purposes. We must ask, Who stands to benefit if this information is accepted as true? Being mindful in these ways puts us on alert against fraud, yet it does not cut us off from learning.

We should also seek alternative views, since this can help us see the limits of our own knowledge. A bit of conventional knowledge—that "Columbus discovered America," for instance—seems simple and true until an alternative is suggested: "Columbus launched a brutal invasion of an already populated continent." This is not just a different way to describe the same events, but a different way of seeing what those events were. If we try out this alternative view, we can look at what passes for conventional knowledge and see that it is, at the very least, contestable.

What is conventional and what is alternative depends, of course, on where you stand. A view that you consider alternative might seem conventional to someone else. Recognizing this relativity of perspectives is part of being sociologically mindful. But there is more to it. Being sociologically mindful, we can also see that these alternative perspectives create the possibility of understanding the world more fully, because they give us more angles from which to view it.

Perhaps by looking for and seriously considering alternative views—and there are always multiple alternatives—we will eventually get closer to a better version of the truth. That is something to aim for. In the meantime, it is wise to consider alternative views because doing so can help us see how competing versions of the truth are created. In this way we can learn more about how others see the world, how we have come to see the world, and what more we might see if we are willing to suffer a bit of uncertainty.

Partial Truth and Inevitable Uncertainty

The student who said, "Anyone can make up numbers," did not want to suffer uncertainty. Perhaps he was afraid that if he let go of what he already believed, he would end up lost, not knowing what to believe. He did not know how to be mindfully skeptical.

Part of what we fear is losing what we think is the truth. If we are sociologically mindful, however, we know that we never possess the absolute, complete truth. What we have is a head full of humanly-created images, representations, and accounts that seem to pretty well make sense of the world as we know it. Why not stand ready, as we see and experience more of the world, to invent or borrow new ways of making sense?

If we can admit that there is more to the world than we have yet seen or experienced—and more than we could see and experience in a lifetime—perhaps we can also say to ourselves, "In anticipation of learning more about the world, as I surely will do, I will treat my current beliefs as provisional and explore alternative ways of making sense of things, because one of these ways might come in handy some day."

To adopt this stance toward knowledge does not mean flitting from one belief to another. It is like the deliberate movement of wading upstream in a river. To move ahead you must take gentle steps, making sure of your footing before you shift your weight forward. You must stay flexible and lean into the current. If you rush or lose concentration, you will end up all wet. So you pay attention, moving mindfully when it makes sense to move.

Being sociologically mindful, we know that we never get to the whole truth about the social world. All the truths that we invent or borrow—all the images, representations, and accounts we come upon—are partial views of a whole that is unknowable because it is always changing in ways that run ahead of our ability to understand. We thus need not fear that new ideas and information will wrest the truth from us. They might, however, give us a larger, more complex, and unruly truth to contend with, and that can be unsettling.

For some people it is scary to think of never being sure of having it right. Imagining that one has it right, now and forever, is comforting. The problem, however, is that other people see things differently, and when conflicts arise, others will neither happily conform to the version of truth that comforts us nor lay down their knowledge to embrace ours. And so, if we want to understand and get along with others, we must be willing to seriously consider their perspectives and to tolerate the uncertainty that comes with this openness.

Perpetual Inquiry and Conversation

I have been recommending a mindful skepticism toward all knowledge—that which we already possess and that which strikes us as new and strange. In this way we can avoid the dead ends of nihilism ("There is no truth. Anyone can make up numbers. You might as well believe what you want.") and fanaticism ("There is only one truth and my people know it! All other beliefs are false or insane!"). These are dead ends because they make conversation pointless and offer no hope of resolving conflict.

A mindful skepticism toward knowledge keeps us inquiring, observing, and trying to make better sense of things; it keeps us trying to create more accurate, complete, and useful representations; it keeps us open to new information; and it keeps us connected to others as we try to do all this. Conversation is both a means to this end and an end in itself—at least it is if we believe that it is better to try to understand others than to ignore or to hurt them. Be mindfully skeptical, then, of all knowledge, including that which I have offered in this book. After fair consideration, take and use what is helpful for making sense and for keeping the conversation going.

Curiosity, Care, and Hope

If you could live forever, would life get boring? Some people might say, "Yes, because it would be the same old thing, day after day, forever." But here is another possibility: Life would get more *interesting* because as one learned more about the world, one would see more complexities, more mysteries, more problems to be solved, and more things to be done. Why might some people see life as holding such great promise? I think it is because they are full of curiosity, care, and hope.

If there is no curiosity about the nature of things and how they work, then the world will seem like a drab backdrop against which life is endured until it is over. If there is no care about anything outside one's self or beyond one's time, then it will seem pointless to worry about things that don't matter for getting through the day. Without hope, it will seem pointless to invest much effort in analyzing the social world. So it seems that we need curiosity, care, and hope to spark a desire to pay attention to the social world, to try to understand it as it is, and to use this awareness to pursue change.

Sometimes the conditions of people's lives do not inspire much curiosity, care, or hope. There might be so much day-to-day hardship and sameness, and so few prospects for change, that people limit their attention to each day's tasks and fleeting amusements. Other people might be so comfortable that they too lose interest in critically examining the world beyond their coccoon of privilege. Under these conditions, people are not likely to develop much sociological mindfulness. Then again, perhaps the process can be turned around. Perhaps a lesson in mindfulness can spark curiosity, care, and hope.

Being mindful that the world is a complex and mysterious place, and that penetrating these mysteries is satisfying, ought to arouse our curiosity. Being mindful of how our actions affect others' experiences of joy and suffering ought to encourage feelings of care. And being mindful of how human action creates the world ought to give us hope that we can make the world a better place. Obviously these are expressions of my own wishes, yet I have tried to do more than put them forth as wishes.

I have tried to show how much there is to be curious about: the many connections, patterns, contingencies, appearances, and inter-dependencies that constitute the social world; all the ways that people try to solve problems together and end up creating cultural habits; the ways that some people create social arrangements to benefit themselves at the expense of others; and all the ways that people create the images, accounts, and representations that make up our knowledge of social reality. We could study these matters forever and always be learning something new.

I have also shown that sociological mindfulness gives us reasons for caring. The more we pay attention to and understand connections, interdependencies, and contingencies, the better we can see how *our* ways of thinking and acting affect *others'* chances for good lives. We can see, too, that what others think and do affects us as well. Being sociologically mindful helps us see how this is true in a way that goes beyond what is obvious in everyday life as we interact with others who are close to us.

And just as we care about the others who are close to us, we can, if we are sociologically mindful, come to care about the distant others whose lives are intertwined with ours. At the least, we can thus see new reasons for caring about the social arrangements that bind us to others, for better or worse.

Perhaps you are thinking, "What about hope? It seems that 'being sociologically mindful' just makes us aware of how messed up the social world is. How is *that* supposed to inspire hope?" Actually, mere awareness of problems—inequalities, exploitation, the suffering of others—is not supposed to inspire hope. It is supposed to inspire outrage and a desire to change things. Unfortunately, when awareness of problems is combined with feelings of powerlessness, the result is often despair.

Being sociologically mindful, however, we know that the social world is, for all its seeming solidity, a social construction. All the ideas, habits, arrangements, and so on that make up the social world are human creations. We know, too, that the social world keeps going as it does because of the beliefs people share and because of how they keep doing things together on an everyday basis. If we are mindful of all this, we can see that the problems that exist now need not exist forever; they are all within our power to overcome.

Of course it will not be easy, because many powerful people benefit from the arrangements that cause problems for so many others. There is also the problem of changing the arrangements that are devised to keep things from changing. Yet the possibility of change always exists, if only people can organize to make it happen, and that is a good reason for hope.

Mindfulness can get us out of the rut of despair by reminding us that we cannot change a society overnight by ourselves. It is silly to say, "I failed to bring about a revolution this week, even though I tried very hard. That proves it's hopeless. I guess I'll give up and just march along with everyone else." Yet many people fall into this kind of trap. The way out is through awareness that change requires working with others to challenge existing arrangements and to create new ones. We cannot do it alone.

There is no point in despairing because we cannot single-handedly change the world. Of course we can't. We can, however, try to find or organize others who recognize a need for change and are willing to work for it. It is amazing how being in community with others can help alleviate the despair that arises from failed dreams of heroism.

Sociological mindfulness also reminds us that we *can* change a small part of the social world single-handedly. If we treat others with more respect and compassion, if we refuse to participate in re-creating inequalities even in little ways, if we raise questions about official representations of reality, if we refuse to work in destructive industries, then we are making change. We do not have to join a group or organize a protest to make these kinds of changes. We can make them on our own, by deciding to live differently.

Perhaps our modest efforts will reverberate with others and inspire them to live differently. Or perhaps no one will notice, or they will notice but think we are strange. And so you might think, "If no one is going to notice that I am a superior moral being, then what is the point? Why bother to be different and risk ridicule?" That is one way to look at it. Being sociologically mindful, however, suggests a different thought: "I cannot be sure that *anything* I do will change things for the better, yet I can be sure that if I do not at least *try*, then I will fail to do what I think is right and will be contributing to keeping things the same. Therefore I will opt to do what is right, whether much or little comes of it."

In the end, sociological mindfulness must be about more than studying how the social world works. It must also do more than inspire curiosity, care, and hope—although these we cannot do without. If it is to be worth practicing, sociological mindfulness must help us change ourselves and our ways of doing things together, so that we can live more peacefully and productively with others, without exploitation, disrespect, and inequality. Sociological mindfulness is a way to see where we are and what needs to be done. It is a path to heartful membership in a conversation that ought to have no end.

RELATED READINGS

Kuhn, Thomas. (1970). *The Structure of Scientific Revolutions* (2nd ed.). Chicago: University of Chicago Press.

Lofland, John, & Lofland, Lyn H. (1995). *Analyzing Social Settings* (3rd ed.). Belmont, CA: Wadsworth.

Maxwell, Nicholas. (1984). *From Knowledge to Wisdom*. New York: Basil Blackwell.

O'Hear, Anthony. (1989). *An Introduction to the Philosophy of Science*. New York: Oxford University Press.

Thomas, Jim. (1993). *Doing Critical Ethnography*. Newbury Park, CA: Sage.

Winch, Peter. (1958). *The Idea of a Social Science and Its Relations to Philosophy*. London: Routledge and Kegan Paul.